# German Armored Trains
# on the Russian Front
# 1941-1944

Wolfgang Sawodny

**Schiffer Military History**
Atglen, PA

## About the Book

While the Soviet Union regarded armored trains as an effective weapon since revolutionary times and soon developed their few armored cars into a standard type strongly armed with artillery, the German military leadership regarded them at the beginning of World War II as an outmoded weapon, and the offensive action of the few such trains which they still had (and which were based on a very different concept—numerous cars, large numbers of infantrymen, few heavy weapons) in the first two war years seemed to confirm this opinion. This changed shortly after the eastern campaign began. On the one hand, the Russian armored trains developed an active and not at all unsuccessful combat application during the German advance, though they suffered heavy losses; on the other, the partisan activity behind the front grew ever more vigorous, attempting to break the German backline supply routes, and provided a new and very important field of operations for the German armored train, that of securing railroad lines. They made a significant contribution to the fact that this "rail war" remained undecided, at least until the summer of 1944. During the withdrawals of 1943 to 1945, they were drawn more and more into the combat events on the front, in which, though, their inferiority to the Russian trains in terms of their being limited to the tracks, having thin armor and insufficient armament, soon became evident. Yet they remained in self-sacrificing service until the last days of the war. This volume seeks to portray the action of the armored trains in the fighting on the eastern front.

## Photo Credits

AG Axel Gutmann, Schwabbruck; BA Federal Archives, Koblenz; HG Helmut Griebl, Laaben, Austria; HW Hansjürgen Wenzel, Koblenz; JM Janusz Magnuski, Warsaw, Poland; JW Jürgen Wilhelm, Margetshöchheim; KM Karlheinz Münch, Schwetzingen; NB Norbert Bartel, Cologne; PM Paul Malmassari, Heidelberg; RF Reinhard Frank, Gilching; SZ Steven J. Zaloga, Stamford CT, USA; all other photos are from the author's collection.

*Picture on page 1: The armored locomotive of the BP 42 or 44 was from Series 57 and was equipped with an extra tender coupled to the front.*

Translated from the German by Ed Force

Copyright © 2003 by Schiffer Publishing, Ltd.

Printed in China.
ISBN: 978-0-7643-1783-5

This book was originally published under the title,
*Waffen Arsenal-Panzerzüge an der Ostfront 1941-1944*
by Podzun-Pallas Verlag, GmbH

We are interested in hearing from authors with book ideas on related topics.

## Bibliography

Anonymous, Eisenbahn-Panzerzug, in "Waffenrevue" No. 20, 1976.
Benussi, G., Treni armati, treni ospedale 1915-1945, Parma 1983.
Caiti, P., Artiglierie ferroviarie e treni blindati, Parma 1974.
Ehrhart, K. & Kopenhagen, W., Panzerzug-Neuauflage 75, in "Armeerundschaü 1976.
Kopenhagen, W., Panzerzüge-Schienen-Dinosaurier oder moderne Militärtechnik, in "Eisenbahnjahrbuch 1977", Berlin 1977.
—, Sowjetische Panzerzüge und Eisenbahngeschütze, Waffen-Arsenal S-36, Wölfersheim-Berstadt 1995.
Magnuski, J., Wozy bojowe LWP 1943-1983, Warsaw 1985.
—, Panzerbetriebwagen Nr. 16, in "Militariä Vol. 1, No. 3, 1992.
—, Pociag panzerny BP-43, in "Nowa Technika Wojskowä No. 10, 1994.
—, Niemieckie pociagi pancerne BP 42/BP 44, in "Nowa Technika Wojskowä No. 3 & 4, 1995.
—, Panzerne wagony motorowe NKWD, in "Nowa Technika Wojskowä No. 9, 1996.
—, Pociag pancerny "Smialy" w trzech wojnach, Warsaw 1996.
Malmassari, P., Deutsche Panzerzüge zwischen 1914 und 1945, in "Modell-Fan" No. 10, 1988.
—, Les trains blindes 1826-1989, Bayeux 1989.
Pozeljujew, W. A., Bronenozy schelesnich dorog, Moscow 1982.
Romadin, S., Bronevaja gvardija revoluzil, in "Model Konstruktor" No. 11, 1989, No. 3 & 4 1990.
Sawodny, W., Deutsche Panzerzüge im Zweiten Weltkrieg, Waffen-Arsenal S-4, Friedberg 1986, 2nd ed. Waffen-Arsenal Highlight Vol. 1, Wölfersheim-Berstadt 1996.
—, Panzerzüge im Einsatz, Waffen-Arsenal S-13, Friedberg 1989, 2nd ed. Waffen-Arsenal Highlight Vol. 2, Wölfersheim-Berstadt 1997.
—, Die Panzerzüge des Deutschen Reiches 1904-1945, Freiburg 1996.
Stabsoffizier beim Kommandeur des Panzerzüge (ed), Panzerzüge No. 1 & 2, 1944, no site.
Trojca, H. & W., Der Panzertriebwagen "Kirowski", in "Modell-Fan" No. 4, 1994.
Trojca, H. & W., (No. 2 also Ledwoch, J.), Panzerzüge No. 1 & 2, Warsaw 1995.
Wenzel, H., Lokomptoven ziehen in den Krieg, Vol. 1-3, Vienna 1977-1980.
Wiener, F., Gepanzert auf Schiene und Strasse, in "Feldgraü Vol. 10, 1962.

Schiffer books may be ordered from your local bookstore, or they may be ordered directly from the publisher by writing to:

Schiffer Publishing, Ltd.
4880 Lower Valley Rd.
Atglen, PA 19310
(610) 593-1777; Fax (610) 593-2002
E-mail: Info@schifferbooks.com

Please visit our website catalog at *www.schiffer-books.com* or write for a free catalog.

Printed in China

# Introduction

After the successful conclusion of the French campaign at the end of June 1940, Hitler hoped he could move Britain to make peace. After this was shown to be an illusion and no alternative to continuing the sea war appeared on that front—the only halfhearted plan to invade Great Britain was soon ruled out by the loss of the air war over the island—, Hitler turned to the enemy whom National Socialism had regarded as one of his chief foes from the beginning, Communism, and especially its embodiment in the Soviet Union. Here it was not just an ideological disagreement between two dictatorial systems, both unscrupulous and inhuman, but also the presumably necessary expansion of the "Lebensraum" of the German "Master Race" at the expense of the Slavic "Untermenschen", which implied measures to wipe out the native population.

On August 28, 1939 Hitler had made an agreement with Stalin, to the amazement of many, that kept his back free for the invasion of Poland, but it was probably clear to both that this was an agreement for a time, which they would keep as long as it was useful, and that each would be ready to renounce or break at the optimal time for him. Of course the Soviet Union had armed itself steadily since 1930, but this process was not yet finished. The results of Stalin's purges in 1937-1939, to which numerous high-ranking officers had fallen victim, were by no means overcome, the lessons of the difficult 1939-1940 winter war with Finland were just beginning to be processed, the production of new and more effective weapons, such as the T 34 tank and the "Katyushä rocket launcher (the feared "Stalin Organ") were just beginning in 1940-1941. A part of these difficulties had not gone unnoticed by the Germans; the taking of Bessarabia and the Baltic states by the Russians in June and July 1940 were seen as a certain threat, perhaps to the Romanian oil fields so important to the Germans, and finally the Soviet Union appeared as Great Britain's only remaining potential European ally for the further waging of the war, and it was believed that the first overtures in this direction could be sensed. In purely military terms one would have to see that—if such an adventure was to be undertaken at all—an attack date in the spring of 1941 was probably the latest possible one that still had a chance of success.

After Hitler had decided to attack the Soviet Union, the military and army high command began in July 1940 to plan the campaign. In the tried and true "Blitzkrieg" form, it was supposed to smash the opposing forces, as much as possible, before the defensive positions on the Dniepr and Duna, then make the decisive breakthroughs and wipe out the rest of the Red Army, in order to engulf Leningrad, Moscow and Kharkov. Then an occupation of the area up to the northern Dvina, the centerl Volga and the Don (later extended to the lower Volga, thus to the Archangel-Astrakhan line) was to take place. The maximum time period was to be seventeen weeks, which would have meant the conclusion of the operation in September if it began in May. At least one of the planners, Generalmajor Marcks, had recognized risks: one was the impossibility of occupying the constantly expanding area thoroughly; another was the question of what was to be expected in the Soviet Union did not crumble under the strikes it suffered in the west, and if Stalin held out behind the Urals and continued the war in coalition with Britain and perhaps the USA. But he too neglected to stress these problems sufficiently—especially to his superiors. The possibility that the timetable might be exceeded considerably and continue the campaign into the Russian winter seems to have turned up briefly, but without being considered seriously. Two further points from the plans might also be noted. Supplying such numerous troops over the ever-increasing distances was naturally of special importance. Aside from their being supplied as much as possible from the conquered areas, there were still enough materials, ammunition and fuel, among other things, that had to be transported by road and rail. The Soviet Union's railroads, though—except for a few lines in the Baltic area and Poland that were taken over in 1939-1940, were wide-gauge (1524 instead of 1435 mm), so that they could not be used by German locomotives and cars. Thus it was presumed that after only about two weeks a transport capacity—still limited—by rail would be available. Since it was not known whether sufficient intact rolling stock would be captured, it was decided from the start to convert the lines to standard gauge, which naturally required work forces and—depending on their numbers—time. It was also assumed that in the hinterlands scattered troops and partisan groups could be active (even though the extent of such subsequent activities could not be imagined). Thus between the backline army zone and that of civilian government by "Reich Commissars" there was to be a "rearward army areä for every army group, with its commander directing three securing divisions (older personnel, lightly armed from captured stocks) to guard the supply depots, supply routes, transport lines and communications links.

On December 18, 1940 Hitler released Directive No. 21 for "Operation Barbarossä, in which for the second and third phases of the campaign discrepancies from the General Staff's concepts appeared in terms of operative action and were not disposed of. In the spring of 1941 the German forces marched to the eastern boundary bit by bit, but the attack date, originally set for mid-May, suffered from the Balkan campaign, which became necessary early in April and, what with the inclusion of Yugoslavia, required stronger forces than originally planned for Operation "Maritä (the occupation of Greece), and was postponed almost six weeks. In the early morning hours of June 22, 1941 the German troops crossed the border into the Soviet Union. Along with them—probably noticed by very few—were the units of a small special troop, namely armored trains (PZ). On the other hand, during the course of the campaign there could hardly have been a Germann division that operated near a railroad line and did not come under fire from a Russian armored train.

*A German armored train in the vastness of the Russian winter (PZ 1 on the Smolensk-Vyasma line in February 1942).*

## The Armored Trains of the Opponents

Although they were not involved in the development of armored trains in the 19th century, the German and Russian Empires had recognized the significance of this weapon, and the two empires were the only countries that possessed such units when World War I broke out. To be sure, this conflict, which usually took place in fixed positions, offered armored trains little change to develop. The situation right after the war was very different. The civil wars which followed the October Revolution of 1917 in Russia took place chiefly in wide open spaces and between mobile units—armored trains and cavalry. Numerous armored trains were combined into units and often covered transport trains of infantry and cavalry units. which swarmed out at the point of conflict and were given artillery support by the trains. It is no wonder that the number of armored trains grew quickly. One year after the October Revolution the Red Army had 23, another year later 59, and when the wars ended in 1921 there were 103 such units. The colorful variety of the early improvised types was soon made uniform. The actual combat type was the heavy Armored Train A, which included an armored locomotive and two armored four-axle gun cars, each armed with two 7.62 cm field guns of the 1902 L/30 type in turrets; they also carried five to eight heavy Maxim machine guns. The crew numbered 162 men, and 23 unarmored cars were included to carry them. These trains were supported by light armored trains, with only single-turreted gun cars, but with larger-caliber (up to 15.2 cm) guns. The Type B had two of them, the type W only one. Trains with even larger calibers (which actually belonged to the railroad artillery) were subordinated to the Navy for coastal protection. In 1926 a confusing renaming was undertaken. The heavy Armored Train A was now—according to the gun capiber—called the light, and the earlier light Type B the heavy, which included the Type W; it could now have two or three gun cars, armed chiefly with the 10.7 cm gun and the 12.2 cm howitzer (with two cars, one 7.62 cm gun could also be present). The heavier railroad guns subordinated to the Navy were now designated Armored Train Type ON (later a new Type W with calibers between 15.2 and 20.3 cm were added). An armored train battalion included two Type A trains and one Type B, plus several partly armored railcars (railgoing armored cars, such as Putilov-Garford, BA 20 or BA 6). The battalions operated independently or were combined in regiments. In the twenties the number of armored trains was reduced; in 1931 there were only about 40 in service (25 Type A, 12 Type B, the rest Type ON), but older types were not scrapped, but only retired, so that they could be reactivated in case of need. In the thirties an expansion of the Red Army took place, also including the armored trains. Around 1935 there were again 60 to 70 armored trains in service, and before the war broke out their numbers had grown to over 80: The Red Army had 53, the NKVD, to which the border troops and railway securing units were subordinated, had 28, and several others with large-caliber guns belonged to the Baltic Fleet; in addition to the increasing numbers, the replacement of older trains can be assumed. The bearer of this increase and renewal was the Type BP-35 Armored Train, and both its light (two turrets with 7.62 cm 02 L/30 or L/40 guns) and heavier versions (one turret with 10.7 cm gun, 12.2 or 15.2 cm howitzer) could be built on the same boxy armored car. An interesting design was that of the 36 two-axle MBW D-2 armored engines with two turrets of 7.62 cm 02 L/30 guns, likewise built in the thirties for the NKVD. Three of them were combined per armored train (of which there were twelve), each with an additional locomotive which brought it to the place of action. The composition of an armored train battalion of the Red Army much resembled the earlier ones. From the revolutionary times to the beginning of the eastern campaign, there had thus been hardly any change in composition, armament and organization of the Soviet armored trains. A compact train (besides the armored locomotive and the two cars with the gun turrets, there were just one or two repulse cars at hand on either end), with high firepower (four guns), was preferred for front use (Type A), while the Type B (two larger-caliber guns with the same number of cars) had support functions.

In the first months of the war, considerable losses were suffered (see below). In order to equalize these somewhat, in the months of August to November 1941 some forty new armored trains were put into service, some of them reactivated trains from revolutionary times, some improvised new constructions in which a technique was utilized that was to become the standard in the future: the use of tank turrets for the guns, at first in wide variety (T-26, T-28, KW01 and -2, and the T-34 as well). At the end of October 1941,

Armored trains from the time of the Russian Revolution and civil wars of 1917-1921 were still used in World War II. Above is a train with open gun positions (with shields), below is the "Krasnoye Sormovö type, named after the factory where it was built; several of these were made. It is seen on the march (locomotive at the front). (HG & JM)

The Armored Train Type BP-35, produced in series on the thirties, is seen above in its light version (Type A) with two turrets per car (7.62 cm 02/L 39 guns) per car, and below in its heavy form (Type B), with just one turret but a larger-caliber gun (here the 10.7 cm M 10 field gun). (AG & NB)

65 new armored trains of the NKPS-42 type were contracted for. These trains were much the same as the BP-35, with simply designed turrets, but fitted with the same gun types and 12.7 mm AA machine guns (after the previously used 7.62 mm Maxim guns, even in quadruple mounts, had proved to be insufficient). It is questionable, though, whether under this designation there were not also trains with four-axle armored cars of the same type, but bearing two T-34 tank turrets, built after October 1941 and later to become the standard type, for which a different type designation has not been found to date. Since with only two of these big gun cars present, one direct hit was enough to put half the train out of action (the greater difficulty of blowing the four-axle cars off the track, though, seems to have been no major argument on the Soviet side), an armored train was designed that replaced each of the two gun cars of that type with two smaller two-axle types, each with one turret of the same type as the NKPS-42, of which the armored train, now designated OB-3, had four in all. How many trains of this type were built is not exactly known; there is only the total figure of 78 newly built armored trains of the NKPS-42 and OB-3 types as of the end of October 1942. The OB-3 armored train was also developed further by replacing the riveted turrets with those of the T-34 tank, and was now designated BP-43; 21 of them were built by the beginning of 1944. Thus from 1943 on, only armored trains with T-34 turrets—with four two-axle or two four-axle (with two turrets each) cars—were built. They were later equipped with an additional four-axle anti-aircraft car, with two 3.7 cm 1939 AA guns in armored compartments—some also had an 8.2 cm M-8 (Stalin Organ) rocket launcher installed bwtween the guns. The exact number of Soviet armored trains in the later war years is not known, but one can presue that it remained high until the war ended. They were organized into armored train battalions, which had only two armored trains, several armored railcars and support vehicles (the former "heavy" armored trains were eliminated). Since 1942 pure anti-aircraft trains were also built, and the Soviets also counted them as armored trains. This must be remembered when one evaluates eastern literature, since German anti-aircraft trains may also be spoken of as "armored trains."

*After the war began, simplified turret designs were adopted. The BP-35 thus became the NKPS-42 (such a car, captured by the Germans, is shown at left, with guns that could also be used for anti-aircraft defense. Similar turrets were used in the OB-3 type of armored train, which had four single-turrett two-axle cars instead of two two-turret four-axle types, to reduce the rate of loss from direct hits. The name "Sovietskaya Armenä shows that this train was stationed in the Caucasus. (below: PM)*

In the immediate prewar era, armored trains were put into service by the NKVD which—though equipped with an additional steam locomotive—had three motorized MBW D-2 motorized cars (two gun turrets each, of the same type as the BP-35). This one was captured in the southern sector of the eastern front in the winter of 1941-42.

Soon the Soviets adopted the simple solution of using tank turrets on the railroad cars. Left: On this car of a BP-35 one of the gun turrets has been replaced by one from a KW-2 tank. The central observation turret has also been replaced by a tank type (A Series?). Right: A captured Russian armored engine with two BT-7 tank turrets.

This "Za Stalinä armored train, probably built in September 1941 (it fell into German hands east of Vyasma that October), was probably a prototype. The installation of T-34 tank turrets, here on a modified BP-35 car (with angled armored walls!), later became the rule for Soviet armored trains (below are the two gun cars of the "Ilya Murometz" armored train in the summer of 1944. The armoring of the locomotive (probably a Series S express type), which was also used later in German PZ 30 armored trains, served as a model for the Series 57 locomotives for the German BP 42 standard armored train. (HW & JM)

*The OB-3 armored train, consisting of four one-turret two-axle cars, was developed further by adding T-34 tank turrets, and was then designated BP-43. In general, though, the armored locomotive was still the Series O freight type used since Revolutionary times. Below: The flak car (two 3.7 cm guns) of the "Moskvä armored train was also of Type BP 43, Lower right: A Russian armored anti-aircraft train with 8.5 cm guns (PM and SZ).*

The German Reich preferred an armored train type that fully complemented the Soviet type. At the beginning of World War I the trains had no fewer than 12 cars and thus were very long. On the other hand, they were manned only by infantrymen; at first there were no guns at all. They were soon reequipped, but only in small numbers and with small calibers (3.7 and 5.2 cm, more rarely 7.5-7.7 cm). This changed only after the war, when securing the new eastern border with Poland and combating internal unrest led to a considerable increase in the number of armored trains to about fifty. With the introduction of the 8.8 cm U-boat gun and arming with light and medium line launchers, a strong armored train was created; besides one to three repulse cars, it included seven to nine gun cars. These Reichswehr armored trains had to be fully disarmed by the end of June 1921 according to the London ultimatum. In the same month, though, the Reichsbahn received permission from the Allies to maintain so-called "rail protection trains" to secure the railways. In addition to the repulse cars, they had six covered freight cars, armored on the inside. With them, they returned to exclusively infantry crews. In 1933, 22 such rail protection trains and five rail protection engines were on hand.

With the expansion of the army from 1935 on, the railbound armored trains were compared with the tank and the aircraft, as well as many other branches of the Wehrmacht, and granted only scant importance. On the other hand, giving them up altogether was not desired, so the seven best rail protection trains of the Reichsbahn were converted to armored trains (PZ 1-7). But only four of them (PZ 3, 4, 6 and 7) were fitted with guns (two 7.5-7.7 caliber guns each). Only they could be used for combat purposes; the other three were merely for railway securing. Thus the traditional multicar trains with relatively light armaments were retained, and this trend was followed until 1942 (see PZ 23-31, 51).

In the occupation of Czechoslovakia in October 1938 and the Polish campaign, armored trains were captured. Out of these, five trains were made up between March and July 1940. While the Czech trains (PZ 23-25), made of six cars each, had their guns reduced to two, in part by removing those already installed, the ex-Polish four-axle cars (PZ 21 and 22) retained both gun turrets. Poland, situated between Germany and Russia, had also gathered much experience with armored trains—in 1921 it has no fewer than 85 of them—and after the Polish-Russian war of 1920 it had closely followed Russian models. The only changes consisted of replacing one field gun with a 10 cm howitzer in the two-turret gun cars and adding a so-called "assault car", an infantry car with radio equipment. These armaments became those of the standard Type 42 German armored train (see below) as of 1942.

The Wehrmacht's early armored trains, adapted from rail protection trains, could be used only on standard-gauge tracks. This is PZ 1, with internally armored freight cars in front and even adapted passenger cars behind the armored Series 57 locomotive.

Although German experience from the first two war years, gained from the—completely offensive—use of armored trains was not very encouraging (of ten such actions in the Polish campaign and the attack on Holland, only two were successful in terms of their intended goals, and even in these two cases the trains were cut off, [p. 9] badly damaged, and had to be relieved by following troops; otherwise one train was lost and two were slightly damaged), and supplying during the Russian campaign was supposed to be done exclusively by road at first, the Inspection of Railroad Engineers (In 10), which still existed then, developed, in the process of its preparations, concepts for two armored train types—PZ 1941 and PZ SP 42, both usable on broad-gauge Russian tracks, while the existing armored trains could be used only after conversion. Thus the In 10 took a new course, ruling out heavy weapons in fixed installations in favor of tanks loaded onto special cars, quickly and easily demounted and reloaded, thus able to work not only as artillery from the trains but also independently in the areas to the sides (these cars were also based on a Polish model). Three of these cars were naturally to be joined by the usual infantry, command cars, etc. Every car was to be individually uncouplable from anywhere on the train. In the 1941 armored train, each one was also to have its own power and thus be usable alone, while a Diesel locomotive was to pull the SP 42. These were very flexible, forward-looking solutions, which offered particularly good perspectives for action against partisans. For the 1941 train, a multiphased action was planned; in the first step (immediate solution), the tanks (captured French Somua S 35 models) were loaded on specially equipped Ommr cars (tank carrier cars) pulled by a steam locomotive (BR 57) with only makeshift armor on the cab. Only this stage was realized before the Russian campaign began, but the OKH insisted that the

trains should also have two cars for infantrymen. These open-top cars had side armor with loopholes, but offered protection only to men lying down, and were totally unfit for use in the rainy autumn season or the cold Russian winter. Since the material originally intended for five such trains was later stretched to six (PZ 26-31), three of them had only two tanks instead of three on suitable cars, and two had only one infantry car instead of two; the sixth train was pulled by a WR 360 C Diesel locomotive. With these units, which scarcely deserved the name of armored trains, Germany went into the eastern campaign. It is no wonder that in the advance phase the crews tried to obtain captured cars from Russian armored trains in order to afford themselves more pleasant living conditions, to the point where PZ 28 came to resemble a complete heavy Russian BP 35 train, including an armored locomotive. Along with these six broad-gauge trains, the standard-gauge trains no. 1-4, 6 and 7 (1 and 2 had acquired two gun cars, the first of only 4.7 caliber) were intended to be used in the Russian campaign, but they could travel into the depths of Russia only after being modified. This array remained unchanged until the end of 1941.

At the beginning of the Russian campaign, the command office of the "Staff Officer of the Railway Armored Trains" was created. For unknown reasons, though, it was not attached to the railway troops, but subordinated to the General of the Fast Troops (later Armored Troops). This must be regarded as a wrong decision, but until well into 1944 the main task of the armored trains was securing rail transport routes against partisan attacks. In front-line combat too, in which they became increasingly involved since the beginning of 1943, the actions of the armored trains were determined more by their being limited to railway lines than by the tactics of motorized troops or tanks. This mis-

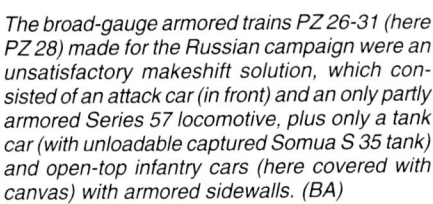

The broad-gauge armored trains PZ 26-31 (here PZ 28) made for the Russian campaign were an unsatisfactory makeshift solution, which consisted of an attack car (in front) and an only partly armored Series 57 locomotive, plus only a tank car (with unloadable captured Somua S 35 tank) and open-top infantry cars (here covered with canvas) with armored sidewalls. (BA)

*An armored train of the standard BP 42 type developed by In 6, twelve of which were put into service from December 1942 to February 1944.*

taken decision manifested itself particularly in plans for new construction. The significant concepts of the Railway Engineer Inspection, including those concerning the constant fighting against partisans, were tabled (only when it was too late were some aspects of them brought up again), and the Inspection of the Fast Troops (In 6) developed its own, very different concept in Armored Train 42. There was no longer any thought of a Diesel locomotive or self-propelled cars; they stuck with the venerable steam locomotive with all its disadvantages (frequent refueling with coal and water, laborious maintenance). They did not want to do without a strong infantry crew, and the artillery was modified. After the Polish model, they installed two 7.62 cm field guns and two 10 cm howitzers (the later BP 44 development even had four 10.5 cm howitzers), and the train thus became more and more of a railway gun battery. Two quadruple 2 cm flak guns, offering high firepower, replaced the single single guns installed before the Russian campaign (which had replaced the earlier twin heavy 34 machine guns), and proved very effective for air and ground action. From the ideas of In 10 they took two tank carrier cars, on which unloadable Czech 38(t) tanks were carried. Along with the two Panhard 38(f) scout cars, which could run on rail or road, they formed a respectable support for the use of infantry against partisans away from the railway line. but they were no longer suited to fight against Russian tanks. The lack of an armor-piercing weapon was a grave defect that was only rectified with the addition of two tank destroyer cars with Panzer IVH turrets (7.5 cm KwK L/48) on BP 44, but its first example was not ready for service until mid-1944 (before that, no longer mobile tanks or antitank guns were often carried on additional low-side cars). The second major problem was the poor armor protection. Since two-axle cars were retained because they were easier to get back on the rails after derailings, the armor—so as not to exceed the axle pressure—could not be thicker than 30 mm, a thickness that was pierced easily by shells fired with high muzzle velocities. On the other hand, these trains were much too elaborate for anti-partisan action; neither heavy armament nor all-around armor was necessary for that. On the contrary, from the summer of 1943 on, when the partisans could no longer be kept away from the railways and natu-

rally were eager to put their enemies, the armored trains, at least temporarily out of action with explosives, then even if only one or two cars were hit, there were much greater losses in material and specially trained personnel. The task of fighting partisans was met just as well by the rail protection trains, built at much less expense and manned by personnel from railway securing units (see below).

But before the first of these new armored trains (PZ 61) reached the front in December 1942, the fleet of armored trains had been increased in other ways. First there were two Polish trains, which the Russians had captured in Povorsk and Lemberg and converted to broad gauge for their purposes. At the beginning of the Russian campaign they fell into the hands of the Germans, who were thus able to fulfill a long-standing request of theirs—and a manner of operation practiced by the Soviets in their armored train battalions almost from the start—the operation of two armored trains together. Thus in February 1942 they, called Kampfzug I and II, were combined into the PZ 10 unit. Of course the shortage of armored trains meant that thay were often used in very different places, which resulted in the disbanding of the unit on August 1, 1943; Kampfzug I remained PZ 10. while Kampfzug II became an independent PZ 11. They were also changed—like all other German broad-gauge armored trains between April and July 1942—to standard gauge, a sign that, with that year's summer offensive from the eastern Ukraine in the direction of Stalingrad and the Caucasus, the Germans were not counting on railway securing in the hinterlands. In May 1942, PZ 25, put out of service in the summer of 1940 and now reactivated, went back into action.

In view of the small numbers of armored trains and the vastness of the railway lines, the units charged with their defense, particularly the securing units, cobbled up what they could. From available vehicles, weapons and equipment they came up with makeshift armored trains (as ordered on July 12, 1943, they were designated "railway protection trains" to differentiate them from the regular armored trains). Their exact number can no longer be determined (the first news of such a—broad-gauge—train came from the latter half of July 1941), their composition varied greatly because of the conditions when they were assembled; very

The further development of BP 42 was the BP 44, first delivered in mid-1944 and armed with four 10.5 cm 18M howitzers in the same turret type. The barrel can be seen behind the 38(t) tank being unloaded. (AG)

An important development to BP 44 was the use of two tank destroyer cars, each with a turret from the Panzer IV H tank.

The command train for the armored train regiment staffs was half of PZ 72 (Type BP 42), divided in the spring of 1944. This is 72B of the Regiment No. 3 staff. (Oberstlt. Dr. Günther)

Two Polish armored trains that fell into Soviet hands in 1939 were captured by the Germans and the start of the Russian campaign and put to use together in the PZ 10 unit. Above is Kampfzug I in a later stage (with a German Series 57 armored locomotive and a heavy Soviet Type BP 35 armored car rebuilt into a command and flak car). Below is Kampfzug II (later separated as PZ 11), still with broad gauge and a Polish Series Ti 3 armored locomotive, shortly after going into service at the beginning of 1942. (AG)

From captured Polish material, this time going straight into German hands in 1939, PZ 21 was made up and sent to the eastern front in October 1942. The boxy German armored locomotive is 93 298.

It replaced PZ 25, made up of captured Czech material and active against partisans since May 1942. On the gun car, a 7.5 cm Skoda D 28 gun was mounted on a platform with low armored walls. In front of it is a flatcar with a captured Somua S 35 tank, in the manner of the broad-gauge Armored Trains 26-31.

*PZ 51, developed from a railway protection train in 1942, used armored Soviet freight cars and four turrets of BT-7 tanks with 4.5 cm guns, and an armored Series 38 locomotive.*

often captured materials, including Soviet armored-train cars, were used. In the railway protection trains the technique, borrowed from the Russians, of using the turrets of—generally Russian—tanks as armament soon appeared. Rearmament of the railway protection trains was frequent when new material was available. Sometimes such protection trains were taken into the ranks of the regular armored trains, such as the "Stettin", composed of Russian freight cars armored inside, carrying four Soviet BT-7 tank turrets (4.5 cm KwK), which went into service in August 1942 as PZ 51 after being under construction since the beginning of that year. In the summer of 1944 the railway protection train "Blücher", having in its last form no fewer than two each of T-26, T-70 and T-34 tank turrets, became PZ 52 after considerable rebuilding. Toward the end of the war such rebuildings became much more frequent. On the eastern front, the former railway protection trains no. 83 and 350 became armored trains, keeping their old numbers, and so did the newly assembled protection train "Berlin" (which carried five Panzer V "Panther" tanks).

Buy back to the standard BP 42 armored train developed by In 6. The twelve trains of this type reached the front between late December 1942 and mid-Fenruary 1944; no fewer than ten of them were sent to the eastern front (the other two—PZ 64 and 65—were also transferred there toward the end of the war). The first three trains of the improved BP 44 type (four 10.5 cm howitzers, tank destroyer cars with Panzer IVH turrets) were being finished in the summer of 1944, but only the first (PZ 73) left the armored train replacement unit, located since the spring of 1942 in Rembertow (east of Warsaw), fully equipped and heading for Italian. PZ 74 and 75 had to be rushed into service, although neither the new guns nor the tank destroyer cars were ready. The next train of the type (PZ 76) was only finished in November 1944, followed by PZ 77-79 in January and February 1945, all going to the eastern front. PZ 80 and 81, finished just before the war ended (PZ 82 was still being built) did not get any farther than Bohemia and Moravia. In addition, almost all the older armored trains were gradually updated to match the BP 42 and later 44 (K.A.N.1169x). These measures were carried out when the trains had to be sent to a repair shop anyway for overhauling or repairing of damage, so they were spread over a broad span of time. The modifications to PZ 6 and 27 in the summer of 1942 already tended in that direction, but did not completely fit into the plan. This took place only with PZ 1 and 23, which were overhauled between the late fall of 1942 and July 1943. The last train thus modified was PZ 25 (September-November 1944; the rebuilding of PZ 2—in progress since July 1944—was halted in November 1944). Available cars were used as much as possible for the flak and command cars, but captured Russian armored train cars, mostly four-axle types, were used as gun cars, with the two gun turrets (now made in Germany) retained but the bodies much changed; PZ 3 and 30, though, were given (naturally four [p. 14] instead of three) single-turret two-axle cars of the Soviet OB-3 (see above) type. The tank-carrier cars, with 38(t) tanks (which replaced the Somua 35 tanks on the just-named trains) and later tank destroyers, had to be built new—when they were not available as with PZ 26-31.

*The gun cars of the protection train "Blücher" were armed in its final phase with Soviet T-34 and T-70 tank turrets. When it was built into PZ 52 in the autumn of 1944, the T-34 turrets were replaced by those of the German Panzer IVH, and the T-70 turrets served only as armored observation posts, while a platform for quadruple 2 cm flak guns was built in the rear ends of the cars.*

For a long time the former rail protection engine remained alone as Panzertriebwagen (PT) 15. It was now used on the eastern front—subordinated to PZ 25—from December 1941 to September 1942. In the advance phase, several of the NKVD trains (see above), consisting of MBW D-2 engines, had fallen into German hands essentially undamaged. Seven of these cars—after some revisions (in particular, the motors and radio sets were replaced, but the two turrets with their 7.62 cm guns were modified only slightly)—were then put into service as the only rolling armored engines, but were always assigned to armored trains. The first—PT 17—joined PZ 61 in December 1943, the last—PT 23—reached PZ 76 in November 1944. They were joined by the Diesel locomotive rebuilt as an armored engine for the projected but never completed SP 42 train (see above) as PT 16 (to PZ 11 in May 1944). These engines, being well-armed separate cars, were much better suited to front-line surprise attacks than the much more ponderous armored trains, and thus provided the latter with a welcome variety and strength.

In 1944 a long-standing request (long practiced by the Soviets) was finally fulfilled, not having been possible earlier for lack of materials. Probably initiated by the successful cooperation of PZ 2 and 68 at the Beresina crossing near Shazilki in November 1943, armored train battalions with two trains were finally to be formed. After it happened again and again that impractical action resulted in losses, armored train regimental staffs were to be set up at the Army Group level to direct these battalions. This was planned for the first half of 1944, and to create the planned command trains for these staffs, PZ 72 was divided into two halves (PZ 72 A and B) in February 1944. The joint operation of the two trains was carried out—when possible—but the establishment of regimental staffs was much delayed by the heavy armored-train losses of that year (per regiment, three two-train battalions were planned, but even later this number was never attained; :regimental battle groups" were spoken of then). Regimental Staff No. 3 )Oberstleutnant Dr. Günther, Army Group Center) began its work only in October 1944, Regimental Staff 1 (Oberstleutnant H.G. Baron von Türckheim, Army Group A) in November 1944.

*The crew of the broad-gauge armored trains 26 to 31, with their open infantry cars fully unsuited to fall and winter service in Russia, tried as soon as possible, by obtaining captured Russian material, to put a roof over their heads. Most successful was PZ 28, which by September 1941 included a complete heavy-type PB-35 including an armored locomotive (above, KM). Others made do with individual cars, such as PZ 26 (lower left), with one of the Revolutionary "Krasnoye Sormovö type (rebuilt as a flak car; behind it—covered with tent canvas—is one of the original infantry cars). PZ 27, which lost its cars at Sukhinitski early in 1942, was reformed with gun cars of the (light) BP-35 type (lower right).*

The armored trains that developed from the railway protection trains (No. 1-4, 6 and 7), like the early broad-gauge PZ 26-31 (and PZ 23-25, made up of captured Czech material), were later revised in equipment and manpower to equal the BP 42 or 44 types, with captured Russian material also used for the gun cars, but in modified form. Above is PZ 31 (light BP-35 cars), below PZ 0 (four OB-3 cars); the gun turrets are German-made. In PZ 30 the infantry cars (with command central and flak stand) before and after the locomotive are rebuilt captured cars of the BP-35 type.

Usually only the chassis of captured Russian cars were used, equipped with new bodies that followed the same pattern—on the low front platform were a turret with a 7.62 mm 295/l(r) gun and an observation post; on the higher rear platform, which showed certain structural variations, was the 10 cm 14/19 (p) howitzer. Above is the car of this type from PZ 1, below that of PZ 26.

15

*Several of the Soviet MBW D-2 armored engines used in NKVD armored trains fell into German hands. Seven of them, after rebuilding (motor, radio, turret-turning mechanism sleeves), were put into service from Decembger 1943 to November 1944 as "armored gun engines" (PT 17-23) and assigned to individual armored trains on the eastern front. (BA)*

*The WR 550 D 14 Diesel locomotive intended for the SP 42 armored train was rebuilt into an armored engine (PT 16) by adding gun platforms for German turrets (7.62 cm F.K. 295/1) on both sides (here equipped with two additional tank-destroyer cars with T-34 turrets). With its powerful motor and 100 mm side armor, it was the fastest and best-armored of the German armored engines. (HW)*

# Action

For the attack on the Soviet Union, first of all the primitive broad-gauge "armored trains" were naturally prepared, with two assigned to each army group. The two of Army Group North (PZ 26 and 30) were in Eydtkau ready to attack in the direction of Kovno, those of the Army Group Center (PZ 27 and 29) were at the Bug bridges in Platerov and Terespol, and PZ 31 was with Army Group South at the San bridge near Przemysl. This army group's other train, PZ 28, which was to advance to Kovel, could not get there from Kholm because of the damaged Bug crossing east of there, but was before Brest-Litovsk with PZ 27, and was to be transferred from there to Kovel only after Brest-Litovsk was taken. This did not take place, so that it also remained with Army Group Center. The previously gained experience was no more encouraging than the simple construction of these trains in terms of front-line action, and so PZ 27 and 28 were not involved in the taking of the Bug bridge at Brest, nor PZ 31 at the San bridge toward Przemysl. Only PZ 29 took part in a hasty attack on the Bug bridge and the taking of the depot in Siemiatyce. PZ 26 and 30 took part in breaking down the border fortifications and supported the advance toward Kovno. The gauge revision that was not yet finished on all the lines of northern Poland and the Baltic states also allowed the use of some standard-gauge armored trains. PZ 6 advanced from Krottingen toward Libau, PZ 1 took Augustovo in a surprise attack, as did PZ 3 at

*PZ 3 stood at the border depot in Prostken on June 22, 1941, ready to advance toward Grayevo. (HG)*

Grayevo, and PZ 2 took part in the border fighting near Malkinia, but soon they had to stay behind and await the gauge revision—which began at once. In the course of the advance in the summer and autumn of 1941, the German armored trains' chief task was scouting and securing the captured railway lines. Especially when these led through the areas of pocket battles, large numbers of prisoners were brought in on them. The armored trains remained with their army groups and were in the following positions before the beginning of the Russian offensive in November-December 1941 (whereby the stationing of the broad- or standard-gauge trains and the distance to the front can be evaluated as a measure of the importance of the approach routes): Army Group North: PZ 30 in the Volkov area southeast of Leningrad, PZ 6 on the Batezkaya lines toward Novgorod and Dno toward Staraya Russa, PZ 26 on the Dno-Novosokolniki crossover; Army Group Center: PZ 29 at Orel toward Tula, PZ 27 at Orel toward Jelez, and PZ 28 on the Orel-Kursk line, PZ 1 on the Minsk-Orsha-Smolensk line, PZ 2 on the Poloz-Vitebsk-Smolensk line, PZ 3 on the Minsk-Bobruisk-Gomel line; Army Group South: PZ 4 in the Dnepropetrovsk-Saporoshye-Chaplino triangle, PZ 7 on the Fastov-Dnepropetrovsk line, PZ 31 on the Kremenchug-Poltava line.

The numerous Soviet armored trains tried to stop the German advance as best they could all along the front, and their attacks were often unpleasant enough, and even successful in the attack on Rostov in October-November 1941, which was finally turned back. The frequent attempts to break out of pockets with the aid of armored trains (Bialystok, Smolensk, Kiev) failed, though. The known losses testify to the intensity of their actions: By the beginning of the winter counteroffensive, no fewer than 47 Soviet armored trains were destroyed (in which the Luftwaffe played a significant role) or captured in a more or less damaged condition, and these statistics are not necessarily complete. One indicator of the extent of the losses is the information on the NKVD trains composed of MBW engines: of the nine trains that were in European Russia, the date and place of loss are known for six; one other, stationed in Korosten, may not have survived either, and all data on the last two are missing, with not even a note of their fate. On the other hand, improvised armored trains were put into use shortly after the war began, and new construction was begun shortly afterward, so that the losses were soon made up.

The Russian winter offensive mainly involved the armored trains in the area north of the Orel. PZ 27 was cut off in Suchinitski early in January 1942 and largely destroyed (a little later it was reconstituted out of captured material in Roslavl), PZ 29 was surrounded west of Kaluga and had to be destroyed by its own crew on January 10 (it was not replaced). The approach route to the halted front curve between Vyasma and Rshev, threatened from north and south and taking the form of a thin tube, was defended successfully in February-March 1942, with PZ 1 and 2 taking part. The Soviet advances also brought other armored trains close to the front and thus into combat. As the 2nd Soviet Advance Army moved across the Volkov and threatened the Tossno-Lyuban line on which it stood, PZ 30 was in danger, and was surrounded and destroyed in March. Farther south, PZ 6 took part in the defense of Staraya Russa and stayed on the line from Dno to there, which took on special importance after the opening of the Demyansk pocket though the line transferred into this projection of the front, until it was towed away in damaged condition in May 1942 (only after a long time was it replaced that August by the new PZ 51). The important line from Dno to Novosokolniki, protected by only weak securing to the east, was covered by PZ 26. And PZ 3 and 27 tried, coming from Novosokolniki and Nevel, tried to preserve the route to the 83rd I.D. near Velikiye Luki, which was without links to the right or left, until they were badly damaged by explosions at the end of May and left the area to the (already existing) railway protection trains. In the south, PZ 4 was already transferred to the Mius front in December 1941 and took part in defesive action there. When the Soviets broke through across the Donets south of Kharkov in January 1942, PZ 31 took part in the—unsuccessful—defense of Losovaya, augmented by the arrival of PZ 28 with the transfer of the 2nd Army to Army Group South to strengthen the northern corner positions at Balakleya, PZ 4 secured the important supply line from Dnepropetrovsk to Stalino, and the new PZ 10 (broad-gauge) with its two trains, arriving at the first of the year, was transferred to Belgorod in April and took part in the defensive fighting there in the following month, while PZ 31 advanced from Kharkov to Kupyansk at the end of May.

The Russian advances in the winter of 1941-42 and the continuation of the gauge revision had resulted in the latter reaching the front in the spring of 1942. Thus the broad-gauge trains were no longer needed and could be rebuilt to standard gauge. This was done to PZ 26 and 27 in April 1942 at Novosokolniki, to PZ 30 at Lyuban in July, and to PZ 10, 28 and 31 at Kharkov in July and August. This last measure shows that the Germans were not thinking of using armored trains, even for securing operations in the hinterlands, during the summer offensive already underway in the south, where a more extensive network of broad-gauge lines awaited them.

*PZ 1 is seen passing the depot of Kruglanken on its way to action at the Suvalki-Augustovo border crossing.*

Pictures from the advance phase of the Russian campaign: Above, PZ 1 with its armored Skoda railcar (captured from the Czechs) (KM). Right: PZ 2, which had added Czech gun cars by now. Below it, seen in the northern sector, is part of PZ 26, already with captured Soviet cars. Below, PZ 30 is seen coming into a depot in that area (BA). At lower right, PZ 6 is on its way to the Baltic area.

Scenes from the 1941-42 winter war: The gun car of PZ 1, then on the Smolensk-Vyasma line. In front is the Austrian-Dutch (Böhler-Siderius) 4.7 cm gun, in back the 2 cm Flak 38, both in open positions. Below, PZ 28, operating with a captured Russian locomotive in the Orel-Kursk area, still has its (open) German infantry wagon. Between them and the tank-carrier car is an additional flat car with Panzer III tanks. PZ 28 was sent to Army Group South along with the 2nd Army on January 15, 1942.

Below: The newly established (broad-gauge) PZ 10 was made up of two armored trains. At left is Train I with its russian locomotive, at right Train II with its Polish one. The two armored trains—originally Polish—fell into Russian hands around September 20, 1939 in Lemberg and Kovel and—modified for broad gauge—used by the Soviet NKVD. On July 7, 1941 they were captured by the Germans in Kopyczynce (south of Tarnopol).

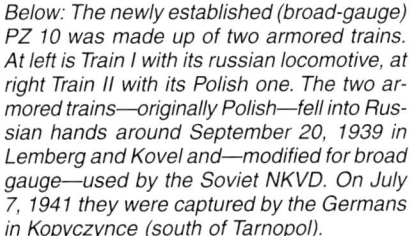

As 1942 began, PZ 27 had lost all its cars at Suchinitzki. It was quickly reconstituted with BP-35 type Russian cars at Roslavl, and was sent to the 83rd I.D. in the Welikiye Luki area on February 22, 1942.

*Along with PZ 27, PZ 3 (above) operated on the Nevel-Velikiye Luki line, which was very endangered by infiltrating Soviet troops and partisans, since early March 1942. On April 22 it hit a mine that destroyed the forward gun car and derailed the next cars (below). On May 15 its locomotive was put out of action by a remote-control mine, and on May 30 PZ 27 also suffered this fate. Both armored trains were then withdrawn for repairs.*

The Soviet armored trains were still very active, especially in the areas involved in the summer offensive, from Stalingrad via Terek and the Caucasus to the Black Sea. The most losses were reported from those areas, but their numbers—certainly not representing total losses—numbered twelve, well under the earlier reports. But on all other front-line sectors too, from Leningrad and Volkov to the area east of Kursk and Kharkov, attacks of these units were reported over and over. From 1943 on the news about Soviet armored trains become remarkably meager. This is not because there were only a few of them, but because they appeared less often. This applies particularly to the Red Army's more frequently occurring advance phases. For the Russian broad-gauge trains had to wait until the rails were adjusted. So it is not surprising that they were heard from only when the front remained static for a long time. In any case, it is known that before the last offensive began in April 1945, the 1st White Russian and 1st Ukrainian fronts each had four armored train battalions, and one can conclude that the forces on the other fronts (corresponding to the German army groups) were similarly equipped.

During the spring of 1942 another task was added to the German armored trains' combat action on the front, and in the next two years it was to become their main one: the securing of the backline railroad lines against sabotage by partisans. Saboteurs were highly regarded in Russian history as well as in Communist theory, and had played a major role in the 1917-1921 Revolution, but had faded into the background because of the expansion of the Red Army in the thirties, so that when the war began in June 1941 there

were scarcely any forces to be used in that way. To be sure, Stalin called in his radio message of July 3, 1941 for the release of an all-encompassing people's war in the areas occupied by the Germans, and the Central Committee of the Communist Party made a resolution on July 18 "about the organization of combat in the hinterlands of the German troops", in which it was particularly advocated "to destroy their connections and transport routes", but putting this into practice at first encountered considerable difficulties, although a not meager number of Red Army men had fled into the woods and swamps in the pocket battles in order to escape being taken prisoner. Party functionaries and members of the Soviet government, who otherwise would have been stood up against a wall by the occupying forces, had joined them. At first, though, any organizational structure was lacking (only on May 30, 1942 did the STAVKA set up a "central staff for partisan movement") as was any material basis (weapons, food, medical supplies), but above all, the essential basis in the population, many of whom saw the Germans as liberators from the Communistic yoke and only gradually realized that they were exchanging the Stalinist regime for the even worse one of National Socialist racism. Thus partisan activity remained scattered and without much effect.

The supply routes, including the railroad lines, remained almost undisturbed. Still, partisan attacks along with the Red Army on the Smolensk-Vyasma railway line in February-March 1942 and Nevel or Novosokolniki to Velikiye Luki from March to May showed their power when directed competently. As of May 1942 the attacks on the railway lines

During the advance phase in the summer and autumn of 1941, numerous Soviet armored trains were destroyed or captured. This picture shows the damage done by a Stuka bomb on a BP-35 gun car. (BA)

Probably also destroyed by an aerial bomb, which simultaneously collaped the bridge, was this heavy railway gun classified as an ON armored train subordinated to the Soviet Navy. (HG)

This railroad battery (an older-type armored train) fell into German hands at the Beresina crossing near Borisov early in July 1941. (JW)

This BP-35 armored train met its fate near Roslavl in mid-August 1941.

In the Kiev pocket, this NKVD armored train made up of MBW D-2 engines came to a halt and was captured by the Germans on September 19, 1941.(JW)

A Russian Flak train from Revolutionary times is seen in a captured depot. On the car in front is an old 7.62 cm L/40 gun; those on the two rear cars (by the signal) have been replaced by the more modern long-barreled version. (HG)

At this backland railroad depot the captured Russian armored trains were assembled.

During the summer offensive, this armored train (above), with tank turrets on a BP-35 car, was destroyed on August 19, 1942. (RF) On the advance to the Volga, an OB-3 armored train (right) fell into German hands. (JW)

A direct hit on a bridge in the Caucasus let the rear half of this OB-3 train fall into the depths. (BA)

This car of an NKPS-42 train was tipped off the tracks. (HG)

*The German increases in 1942 were not significant except for the already noted PZ 10. At the end of May, the reactivated PZ 25, consisting of insufficiently armored Czech cars, was turned over to Army Group Center (above). In October it was already exchanged for PZ 21 (center), which was formerly stationed in France. In terms of armor and artillery, it was better equipped (captured Polish material), but it had the armored locomotive of PZ 25 (93 298). In addition, as of August the Army Gtoup North received PZ 51, made from a railway protection train (below), with four Soviet BT-7 (4.5 cm tank gun) tank turrets. These armored trains still corresponded largely to the conceptions of the Railway Engineer Inspection In 10, which was responsible for the establishment of these units until the autumn of 1941.*

took place mainly in the area from Molodechno-Velikike Luki to Gomel-Bryansk, and inspired countermeasures. On both sides of the tracks, open areas a hundred meters wide were cleared of barriers, depots, bridges and such were secured by fortified support points, which were also set up within sight of each other on especially endangered stretches. The transport trains, often running together in convoys, were accompanied by armed troops and included advance cars to explode mines. The role of the armored trains (and of the railway protection trains now set up to a considerable extent by the securing units) was to patrol the tracks at irregular intervals, accompany important transport trains bring repair crews and combat units to the scene quickly, and protect repair work. To pursue partisan bands, but also to spot them quickly in the field, partisan-fighting commands were set up by the armored trains and were able to operate away from the tracks, along with unloaded tanks and armored scout cars. But fights were relatively rare; the partisans avoided confrontations with the armored trains and their unloaded troops when they could, for their very presence scared the partisans away and fulfilled the purpose of securing the tracks. All these means resulted in a decrease in partisan attacks on the railway lines in the last quarter of

1942, and they remained on a low level in the first two months of the following year.

The locations of the armored trains with Army Group North remained unchanged in the first half of 1942: PZ 30 between Leningrad and Volkov, PZ 51 Dno-Staraya Russa and PZ 26 Dno-Novosokolniki; around the year's end PZ 30 (December 1942) and 26 (January 1943) were taken away for rebuilding. In Army Group Center, PZ 1 secured the Orsha-Smolensk-Vyasma line but was often sent into combat on the line from Vyasma to Rshev, notably in August and November. At the end of November it was badly damaged and replaced by PZ 27, which had just returned after being repaired. The reactivated PZ 25, along with the soon-withdrawn Armored Engine 15, secured the Pripyet line from Luniniec as of May 23, 1942, but was transferred to Polotsk on October 10, 1942 after being repaired, replacing PZ 3. PZ 25, exchanged for PZ 21, went to [p. 29] France, while the latter was first on the line from Borissov to Orsha, but during the attack on the front-line arc of Rshev in November-December it was used in the Durovo-Vladimirskoye area. At the end of December, Army Group Center received the first of the new standard-type BP 42 armored trains, PZ 61. It was stationed in Polozk to secure

The results of partisan activity against the railways. Upper left: Here the rails were simply loosened and removed for some distance, so that the Series 57 locomotive of a supply train was derailed. Upper right: On the Roslavl-Bryansk line a mine explosion threw loco 56 2420 of a furlough train off the tracks. Below: For the same reason, loco 55 4321 of a transport train from the Roslavl works was thrown on its side. Next: A crew recruited from native workers has reached this derailed Series 57 locomotive on the Pripyet line (the loco of the relief train from Luniniec is at left). Bottom: A strong work command has almost heaved this locomotive, 52 019 of the Sfolbunov works (West Ukraine), back onto the rails. Here too, the relief train is seen in the background.

*Above: A bridge blown up by partisans. Beside it: PZ 2 on a securing run. These usually led to small encounters with partisans, scaring them away from the tracks. Below: PZ 3 fires on a village in which partisans are believed to be. Next: They usually had to be sought away from the tracks. Hence the motorized armored vehicles—here a Panzer 38(t) unloaded from PZ 66—were very useful. Bottom: The Panhard 38(f) armored scout cars assigned to the armored trains for reconnaissance as of 1942 were also very effective, as they could run both on the rails (at left, that of PZ 4 at the Rshaniza depot on the Roslavl-Bryansk line) and on the road (at right, that of PZ 2 hunting for partisans).*

Upper left: A partisan-hunting command of PZ 4 in the wooded area northwest of Bryansk. Upper right: This battle group of PZ 1 returns from a swampy area of the central zone with a captured partisan (third from right). Center: A large anti-partisan undertaking includes PZ 2. The villages which could not be occupied constantly were burned without regard for the civilian population, so partisans could no longer use them as bases.

Partisans captured by PZ 3 in the Nevel-Velikiye Luki area.

Often partisans were simply shot or—as here—hanged. But the partisans rarely took prisoners, but killed the Germans who fell into their hands, as well as cooperating countrymen, often after severe punishment.

With their increasing numbers and improving equipment, the partisans always struck back more strongly, and the German armored trains sent against them became favorite targets of their attacks. Above: The Panzer 38(t) of PZ 66 hit a mine during partisan action. Upper right: Fallen crewmen of PZ 63 are being brought back after such an attack. Center: A remote-control mine struck the locomotive of PZ 3 and put it out of action.

On October 7, 1943 PZ 21 hit a mine between Rechiza and Vassilievici, derailing the front half of the train. Here restoration work has already begun.

the line toward Nevel, while PZ 3 took over the line from there to Vitebsk. Early in April 1942 PZ 2 had left for the Bryansk area, where partisan activity was especially strong; there it was supported as of July 1 by PZ 4, turned over by Army Group South. This group, renamed Army Group B at the beginning of July, had to deal with increasing partisan activity in the area (Gomel-Bryansk) adjoining Army Group Center. Thus in July PZ 7 was stationed on the Bakmasch-Voroshba line, followed early in November by PZ 10 (Bakmasch-Gomel) and PZ 28 (Voroshba-Lgov).

But they did not remain there for long. On November 19, 1942 the Soviets began their offensive northwest and south of Stalingrad, enclosing the 6th Army after just three days. On November 23 the newly arrived Army Group Don , set up to stabilize the front west of the enclosing ring, was assigned PZ 7 and 10 (with both trains), and a bridgehead was established in Tchir. This could be held through a month of costly combat. On December 16 the Soviets penetrated the 8th Italian Army and streamed southward. To protect the Donets crossings, PZ 28 was sent by Army Group B and took a position near Kalitva. Sfter the Russians had taken Tazinskaya, a support point vital to Stalingrad, in a surprise attack on December 24, PZ 10 and 28 took part in its recapture four days later. The first half of January 1943 saw all three armored trains involved in the withdrawal combat on the Donets (Belaya Kalitva). Then PZ 10 secured the railroad lines at Likaya, while PZ 7 and 28 covered the withdrawal of the 1st Armored Army to Rostov, from which they later kept the lines west of the city open until Rostov was evacuated (February 9-11, 1943).

These three armored trains took part in withdrawal fighting in the Donets basin (now again with the Army Group South reformed by combining the Army Groups B and Don), typified by the focal points of Artemovsk-Lonstantinovka, Debalzevo and Krasnoarmeysk, and finally Sinelnikovo, which PZ 7, along with alarm units, was able to prevent the Russians from taking on February 19-20. The new PZ 62 arrived in Krasnograd on February 18, just in time for the counterattack, and two days later it took part in the first advance of the SS "Das Reich" Division toward the south. Then it carried on withdrawal fighting along the Poltava-Lyubotin line, until it could advance in the process of regaining Kharkov in March. PZ 7, 10 and 28 at first remained in the Donets basin to secure the tracks, but on April 30 PZ 7, and on June 1 PZ 10 with both its trains, had to be moved back to the Kovel-Korosten-Kiev lines, now strongly endangered by partisans, in the area of the Wehrmacht's Ukrainian Command, where PZ1 had already been with Army Group Center since March.

This was a result of the partisan attacks on the railways, which increased greatly since March 1943, and now took place not only in the focal area behind Army Group Center, but were also spreading out into the neighboring regions. Now modern time-fuse mines with a wide range of various settings were used, and the principle of destroying the tracks along some length of track by a series of explosive charges was used. In the Army Group Center area, there were two focal points for the armored trains. One was

the Polozk-Vitebsk-Nevel triangle, in which PZ 3 and 61—as well as the rail protection trains already there—took part in a succession of large operations from late January to early April, trying to get the better of the partisans. But PZ 3 had to be transferred to Sebesh, as the line from Rositten to Novosokolniki was also being attacked. In several explosive attacks it was finally so badly damaged that in mid-July it was sent home for repairs (and complete rebuilding). In the adjoining area to the north, around Dno, PZ 51, the only armored train still with Army Group North, was faced with growing partisan activity. On the other hand, it was still calm in the area south of Leningrad, where the new PZ 63 arrived early in May 1943. Only from early June on did the partisans in the Volkov area become more active, requiring its action, until the beginning of October, wher it was transferred to Pleskau for the same activities.—The other focal point was the heavily partisan-infested area around Bryansk, in which PZ 2 and 4 tried until the summer of 1943 to offer help as best they could.—At the start of the ongoing removal of the Vyasma-Rshev front-line arc, PZ 21 and 27, which were there, were already transferred away early in February. PZ 27 stayed with Army Group Center for partisan action, at first on the Minsk-Orsha line, later in the Shlobin area. PZ 21 was sent to Kursk to support the retreating 2nd Army. In the combat around this city it was damaged, requiring time out for repairs at Kiev. Then it was on the Kiev-Korosten line (see above), and on April 14 it returned to the 2nd Army and was stationed on its south wing in Sumy or Basy.

The German armored trains were not involved in the front arc at Kursk (July 1943), but all the more in the Soviet countermoves, which were also accompanied by the so-called "rail war", a particularly strong partisan attack on the railway network in the hinterlands. meant to interrupt the arrival of reserves. The first to get into combat was PZ 2, which was involved in vigorous withdrawal fighting on the Bryansk-Dudorovsky line from July 15 on. Soon the Soviets threatened the Bryansk-Orel line, which could be kept open with difficulty with the help of PZ 2 and the hastily summoned PZ 61. PZ 61 then covered the withdrawal along this line to the new position before Bryansk and then (8/19) went back to the 3rd Army. PZ 2 had already been transferred to Unetsha, where it was urgently needed to fight against partisans. PZ 21, already driven out of its station at the southwest corner of the Kursk arc on August 9-10 by the southern Russian advance, moved via Khutor-Mikhailovski (8/11) to the Desna bridgehead at Vitemlya (8/31). Unetsha, Gomel (action on the line to Bakhmatsh on 9/12-17), and finally Vassilievichi (9/25). PZ 4 stayed in Shukovka (northwest of Bryansk) until the Russians advanced north of there, and then went back to Unetsha (PZ 2, which was there, was transferred to Bobruisk). PZ 61 took part in the defenses before Smolensk in the direction of Yelnya, until the first town had to be given up on September 24. The vigor of the partisan rail war in the hinterlands of Army Group Center, which let up only on October 1943, led not only to numerous hasty restationings of armored trains in that area, but also to all usable armored trains be-

*The armored trains that fought on the line from Donets to the Tshir bridgehead and then in the Donets basin after Stalingrad was surrounded: Above: PZ 7 still had the "freight-train look" of the Reichsbahn's old railway protection trains. (BA) Next, the double unit of PZ 10, above Train I, below it Train II (separate Armored Train 11 as of July 1943). At the bottom, PZ 28 with its unloadable captured French Somua S 35 tank.*

Early in July 1942, PZ 4 was transferred from Army Group South into the partisan-threatened Bryansk area. Above: PZ 4 at its new station in Shukovka. On the gun car are two octagonal turrets. The lower front one has a 4.7 cm gun, the back one (with the arched ammunition bunker in between) has a 7.5 cm Infantry Gun 18. At the end of the car is an observation turret. The 2 cm flak gun was installed on the former rail protection car behind it.

During the transfer trip, PZ 4 was hit by a bomb in the Bryansk depot (left). The same fate awaited PZ 1 at the Vyasma depot on December 12, 1942. (right).

PZ 27, almost completely rebuilt after the explosion (only the locomotive remained from the old train), partly with material from a rail protection train, reached Rshev via the line from Vysama in November 1942.

*In December 1942 the first armored train of the standard type developed by In 6 (PZ 61, top picture) was ready for action and was assigned to Army Group Center. The second (PZ 62, middle picture) was delivered to Army Group Don/South in February 1943, at just the right time to begin the counteroffensive in the kharkov area. The third (PZ 63, bottom picture) reached Army Group North in the Leningrad-Volkov area in May 1943.*

ing sent there: the new armored trains of the [p. 32[ standard series, PZ 66 (8.17), 67 (early October) and 68 (11/16) as well as the rebuilt PZ 1 (8/23), while PZ 4 was withdrawn for rebuilding after being damaged in November. Although the number of partisan attacks had decreased since the late summer, they remained at a high level until May 1944. Above all, they were directed more and more at the armored trains, whose movements they tried—probably informed of their movements by Russian railroad men—to cripple by setting off bombs. Partisan reports in the literature cite large numbers of losses in armored trains, which are not correct. Not a single armored train nor—as far as we know—any railway protection train, was ever actually destroyed by them, but there was frequent damage (usually affecting only one to three cars), with losses of men and materials. Usually, though, the trains could be repaired quickly or even stay in service with reduced fighting power.

On October 9, 1942, the Red Army went on the offensive in the Nevel area, since the Army Group North was beaten, and quickly gained ground to the west and south. PZ 61 (to which the first of the new armored engines, PT 17, was assigned as of December) operated north of Vitebsk and PZ 67 northeast of Polosk could not prevent the fall of these two cities into Russian hands or keep the line between them open—not for normal traffic because the enemy was so near, but for their own actions.

In the zone of Army Group South, after successful breakthroughs, as of July 18 PZ 28 moved to Slavyansk and PZ 62 to the Mius front a little later. But soon they had to be called to the Kharkov area, for as of August 3 the Red Army broke through the front west of Belgorod and quickly gained ground to the southwest. On August 6 PZ 62 saw the withdrawal slowed near Solochev (northwest of Kharkov), but on August 8 it had to be removed for repairs. On the same

Unlike the first delivery early in 1943, in which the new-type armored trains were divided evenly among the army groups, the next three that were sent to the eastern front, under the impact of the "rail war" unleashed by the partisans in the summer of 1943, were all sent to the hard-hit Army Group Center: PZ 60 (top) in August, PZ 67 (second) early in October, and PZ 68 (third) early in November 1943.

At the end of August 1943 the first older armored train, PZ 1, rebuilt according to BP 42 guidelines, returned to the front with Army Group Center.

*In October 1943 the Army Group South also received a train rebuilt according to these guidelines, PZ 31, which was lost after somewhat more than two months.*

day, PZ 28 attacked and fought [p. 34] the Soviets, who had broken through at Bogudukov, from the direction of Lyubotin. This train also had to depart with damage on August 16. Finally, Train 10b, now an independent PZ 11, was called in from the western Ukraine. From Kovyagi it attacked the Soviet tanks that had crossed the line from Lyubotin to Poltava and was able to drive them back. It stayed west of Kharkov until August 22, when that city had to be abandoned. Then it had to go for repairs, and the now-repaired PZ 28 was then stationed in Vodolaga (south of Kharkov). As of September 11, PZ 11 and 28 covered the retreat along the line from Chaplino to Dniepropetrovsk and then secured the Dniepr west of that city, but on September 23, PZ 28 was transferred to the Saporoshe bridgehead. PZ 62 moved from its repair shop in Poltava to the Snamenka area.

In September the Soviets were still able to extend several bridgeheads over the Dniepr. The one nearest to Dniepropetrovsk was defended by PZ 11. The Red Army made a breakthrough west of Krementchug on October 15, quickly gaining ground to the south. PZ 62 covered the left flank east of Koristovka, while on October 19 PZ 11 underwent heavy fighting near Pyatichatki and was badly damaged. Meanwhile PZ 28 had been brought in from the abandoned brodgehead at Saporoshye and moved into the combat from the south. It took part in the succession of changing fights in the Krivoy Rog-Doninskaya area, until in January 1944 it was damaged and had to to go to the EAW inNikolayev. In the Snamenka area on November 17, the repaired PZ 11 relieved PZ 62, which was transferred briefly to Kherson. Soon it moved on to the Bobrinskaya area. In December it took part in the withdrawal fighting against the

Russians, who were advancing along the Koristovka-Snamenka line in the direction of Bobrinskaya; then on December 21 it was sent to Rovno in the western Ukraine. On November 3 the Soviets also broke out of the Dniepr bridgehead north of Kiev. Three days later they occupied the Ukrainian capital, one day after that they were in Fastov and on November 13 they advanced to Shitomir. PZ 7, stationed in Korosten, was involved in the defensive fighting on the line from Kiev to there. The front was successfully stabilized through a counterattack; on its right flank the rebuilt PZ 31, stationed in the Smerinka-Kasatin area since mid-October, advanced along the Popelnya-Fastow line, while the newly arrived PZ 69 followed the German troops from Berdichev to Shitomir and secured the lines further in the direction of Korosten. Further to the north, the Soviets were on the offensive going northwestward, and there they met the southernmost unit of Army Group Center, the 2nd Army. On November 15 they crossed the Kalinkovici-Gomel railroad line. The newly arrived PZ 68 was badly damaged in its baptism of fire near Vassiliavici, but remained in service. Along with PZ 2, it was then in the area of the Beresina crossing near Shazilki. This successful cooperation with mutual aid resulted in the German efforts to operate two armored trains in a battalion whenever possible.

In the Army Group South, the Soviets advanced again east of Shitomir on December 24, 1943. They quickly gained ground to the west (see below); to the south, PZ 69 moved off to Berdichev, while PZ 31 rolled unsuspectingly into the Kasatin depot, which was occupied by the enemy, on December 28 and had to be surrendered. In this direction the Russian advance could be stopped again, although large

*PZ 7 was still in its old form, but with an added low-sided car (far right) carrying a tank (Panzer III J?); it fought partisans in the Korosten area since April 1943.*

*The brunt of the armored train action in the southern sector of the eastern front was borne by PZ 11 (above) and PZ 62 (below, with an unloaded 38(t) tank) since the summer.*

units were surrounded near Korsun and Kirovgrad. South of the former (Kristinovka-Talnoye), PZ 62, hastily called in from the Cherson-Nikolayev area, was operating, [p. 35] and southward the newly arrived PZ 70 arrived at the end of Decvember. Only the Soviet offensive that began early in March had a penetrating effect. PZ 62, which crossed the Bug near Ladychin, was able to get away to the west, but PZ 70, which crossed the Bug near Pervomaisk, was no so lucky. At first it fought in the area west of Slobodka, but during that month it had to withdraw ever farther to the southeast into the 6th Army's area (now subordinated to Army Group A). On April 4 it reached Rasdelnaya. When the Russians stormed that town, all the exits were blocked and PZ 70 had to be blown up. On February 21 the 6th Army received the fully rebuilt PZ 30 at Nikolaiev. When the Russians attacked early in March, it saw action north of there and was badly damaged. Since no more repairs could be made in Nikolaiev (PZ 28, which had been at the workshop there, had been evacuated already), it slowly headed back toward Odessa. The withdrawal via Rasdelnaya and Tiraspol ended late in March, since the line was hopelessly occupied. Between April 6 and 8 it had to withstand heavy fighting west of Odessa again, until on April 13 it was the last train to cross the Dniestr-Liman on the ferry and get home via Romania and Hungary, a path already taken by

the not yet completely finished PZ 28. On the north wing of Army Group South the Russians moved fast with breathtaking speed. Korosten fell into their hands on December 29, 1943, Olevsk on January 3, 1944, and Sarny on January 10. PZ 7 offered constant resistance despite repeated damage, which made its return from Sarny to Germany (for total rebuilding) necessary. PZ 10, formerly stationed in Sarny, had already withdrawn to Kovel. Farther south, the Russians broke the Kovel-Kasatin line east of Shepetovka on January 8 and turned to the Proskurov-Smerinka line, on which PZ 62 was active. The Rovno-Shepetovka line was covered by PZ 11, stationed at Rovno, and PZ 71, just arrived on January 12, before both had to withdraw to Zdolbunov at the end of the month and Dubno early in February. After the front had quieted down and the partisan activity had grown much heavier in the Lemberg-Tarnopol area, PZ 11 fought against them on the Krasne-Brody-Dubno line, PZ 71 in the Zbaraz-Tarnopol-Maximovka triangle, and the training train of the Armored Train Replacement Unit— PZ 60 or "R"—was even called in for reinforcement on the Lemberg-Sapiezanka line. At the end of February the Soviets took up the offensive again and advanced far to the south east of Tarnopol. PZ 69 was able to move easily from Proskurov to the Zbrucz crossing near Podvolocyska, where it joined PZ 11 on March 3. As of March 6, they drew back

*On February 21, 1944 the rebuilt PZ 30 was sent to Nikolaiev. It had gun cars of the Soviet OB-3 type, and its flak and command cars were rebuilt from Russian BP-35 cars.*

As 1943 turned to 1944, Army Group South was sent the last three armored trains of the BP 42 series: PZ 69 in November, PZ 70 in December 1943, and PZ 71 (above) in January 1944. (HG)

toward Tarnolpol, having to break through several groups of enemy forces along the tracks. As of March 4, PZ 71 was engaged in heavy fighting near Zbaraz, suffering serious damage. PZ 60/R took its place on March 7, but soon had to withdraw to Tarnopol. All four armored trains (including the patched-up PZ 71, which returned soon) remained active around Tarnopol; but when this city was surrounded on March 24, not one was still there. On March 17, PZ 17 had been sent to accompany replacement troops for Kovel (see below), on March 18, PZ 11 had been sent to Rudnya (near Brody), on March 22 the badly damaged PZ 60/R had left, and PZ 69 was halted, after a vigorous fight, by an explosion during a Russian attack east of Tarnopol, and then shot down. The Russians, who had broken through to the south east of Tarnopol, set out to encircle the 1st Armored Army. PZ 61 was sent from Proskurov via Jarmolinzy to the Husiatyn-Czortkov area, but pushed into the Stanislau area farther west. It was subordinated to the 1st Hungarian Army there, took part in their counterattacks in the direction of Delatyn in the first half of April, and then stayed with them on the line to the Tatar Pass, which led to Hungary. Further to the north, the Soviets had surrounded Kovel on March 16, which even the action of PZ 10 near Maczieyov could not prevent. It remained in Kovel and was almost completely destroyed by bombs and artillery. In the Army Group Center, which was assigned to the Kovel area anyway, this advance awakened the fear that it could continue in the direction of Brest-Litovsk and cut off the most important supply

depots there. In great haste, almost all the army group's armored trains were gathered there: to Brest, where PZ 27 was already, came PZ 1 and 2 on March 18, PZ 66 one day later, and on the Pripyet line PZ 21 was sent to Drohiczxyn, later to Zabinka, PZ 28 to Kobryn. On March 19 PZ 27 undertook a reconnaissance trip in the direction of Kovel; on the night of March 20-21 it was cut off by Russian troops near Zablocie, and a relief attempt by PZ 2 failed. The crew gave up the badly damaged PZ 27; on March 23 they were able to escape from Russian hands during a counterattack with the help of PZ 66. PZ 71 covered the advance of the relief forces from Kholm to Kovel, where they were able to break the surrounding ring on April 5. Army Group Center could now send the armored trains back to partisan fighting in their regular areas: PZ 1 to Ossipovici (Minsk-Bobruisk line), PZ 2 to the Krolevchisna-Glebokie area (Molodechno-Polozk line), PZ 66 to Beresa-Kartuska, PZ 68 to Parokhonsk near Pinsk, while PZ 21 stayed on the line from Brest toward Pinsk.

In the Army Group North, the Soviets had been able to gain a narrow land link to Leningrad in the far north, but otherwise the front—except for the abandonment of the line to Demyansk in the spring of 1943—had remained stable since 1942. Only in the late autumn of 1943 did the Russian breakthrough in the Nevel area cause problems, which grew greater as the army group's boundary was stretched farther and farther to the south. On January 10, 1944 the Polozk area was added to it, through which it "inherited" PZ

PZ 10, which was surrounded and destroyed by bombs and artillery in Kovel in March 1944, is seen earlier in the western Ukraine.

The Army Group North's armored trains are seen at the depot in Farinovo (south of Polozk) during inspection by the staff of Armored Train Regiment 2 (Oberstleutnant von Türckheim). In the foreground is Command Train 72B, parallel to it at left (with three 38(t) tanks in between) is PZ 26, seen mostly as a dark mass because of its camouflage. To its right is a barracks train, behind it—just visible (plume of smoke) is PZ 67. Lower left: During this inspection are, left, Hauptmann Hoppe (commander, PZ 26), center, Oberstleutnant von Türckheim, right, Leutnant Sitzius (commander of PZ 72B), behind him Hauptmann Fischer (commander of PZ 26). Lower right: At the same time, the armored trains of Army Group Center were inspected by the commander of Armored Train Regiment 3, Oberstleutnant Dr. Günther. Here he is talking with Hauptmann Piersdorff (commander of PZ 66, second from right). At the left rear is Command Train 72A.

PZ 2 still looked like this, as it had entered the war in September 1939, in the spring of 1944, after it lost its gun cars that were added later and before it became the last of the earlier rail protection trains to be recalled and rebuilt early in June 1944.

677 there. In mid-January 1944 the Russiand opened [p. 38] their offensive against this army group. For the armored trains, the advance from Novgorod to the west was the target of their action. PZ 63, moved in from the Pleskow area, attacked near Nachtchi on January 18-19 and fought its way back to Bateskaya. When the Russians crossed the Dno-Bateskaya rail line at the end of January, PZ 63 was in action on the north flank near Peredolskaya, PZ 51 in the south near Utorgosh. But soon PZ 63 had to withdraw via Luga toward Pleskow, where it was damaged by artillery fire on March 31 and then left for the hinterlands to be repaired. PT 51 also retired via Dno in the Pleskow area. On February 20 the rebuilt PZ 26 was sent to Asrmy Group North. Around the clock, PZ 26, 51 and 67 now corvred the Rositten-Idriza and Dunaburg-Polozk lines. The Army Group Center also made attacks that required the action of the armored trains; early in February PZ 61 was fighting south of Vitebsk; at the end of the month PZ 66 was active on the north flank and PZ 1 to the south of the Dniepr bridgehead, won by the Russians, near Rogachev. April through June were filled with efforts to overcome the constantly increasing partisan danger through large-scale encirclements. The first of these actions took place in the Lepel area starting on April 16. PZ 26 and 67 (Army Group North), plus 2 and 61 (Army Group Center) and several railway protection trains, formed a barrage line along the Molodecho-Polozk tracks to stop the partisans, who were to be driven toward it. This had only moderate success; the partisans escaped to the south. Thus a further operation, beginning on May 22, saw PZ 21, 28 and 61 under the command of the designated regimental commander, Oberstleutnant Dr. Günther (Command PZ 72A; the other planned holder of this rank, Oberstleutnant Baron von Türckheim, also made an inspection trip to the armored trains of Army Groups North and Center at that time), in a new barrage ling along the Minsk-Bobruisk tracks. The Army Group Center also had PZ 1 (Ossipovici-Chlobin line), PZ 2 (Molodechko-Polozk line, then sent for rebuilding early in June), PZ 66 (Brest-Litovsk-Baranovici line), PZ 68 (being repaired) was on the Pripyet line, where PZ 71 also filled in for a time in May before it was sent to Romania for repairs and improvements.

On the third anniversary of the war against the Soviet Union, the Russian major offensive began against Army Group Center, which had taken up a new phase of the railway war against partisans shortly before; their intensity had practically brought the whole Baranovici-Vilna-Dunaburg line to a stop. [p. 39] Of the armored train group that set out toward Bobruisk on June 23, PZ 21 and 28 suffered mine

*The Soviet 1944 summer offensive against Army Group Center also required sacrifices by the armored trains. PZ 61 (top, with Armored Engine 17, which shared its fate, behind it) and PZ 1 (center) were surrounded in Bobruisk and had to be blown up there on June 27, 1944. PZ 28 (bottom), now with a fully armored locomotive (left edge of picture) and Soviet 7.62 cm ZIS-3 gun on the former repulse car (ammunition bunker and searchlight on the rear part of the car), was lost east of the Beresina crossing near Borissov on June 29.*

damage and had to go back to Minsk. Only PZ 61 (with PT 17) could help PZ 1 south of Bobruisk, but both were surrounded in that city and had to be blown up. PZ 28 fared no better; after makeshift repairs, it opposed the Rssian breakthrough before Borissov. PZ 67 (Army Group North) was in action east of Polozk on June 23, and on June 26 it encountered a Soviet tank attack south of there, was badly damaged, and had to go to Riga for repairs. In its place, PZ 26 was sent to Polozk and withdrew, fighting all the way, to Bigosovo on the Latvian border early in July. In the Pripyet area the rebuilt PZ 68 was not able to keep the Baranovici-Luniniec line open. The danger to Baranovici caused PZ 66 to advance to Byten; after that city fell on July 8, both trains moved slowly back to Brest-Litovsk. PZ 21, stationed in Lida, moved into endangered Vilna on July 6, but could not escape being encircled there; the damage it suffered in action required withdrawal. As of mid-July the Russian offensive spread into the bordering areas. PZ 26 was attacked by Russian tanks near Bigisovo and, after another battle west of Dunaburg, had to go to Riga for repairs. PZ 51 moved back to Rositten. Farther south, PZ 21 and the newly arrived PZ 3 took part in the defense of Kovno (July 22-31), but at that time a gigantic gap in the front was formed, letting the Russians push westward unhindered; later they turned northward, and on August 1 they reached the Baltic Sea near Tukkum, cutting off the entire Army Group North. PZ 67 headed south from Riga via Mitow on July 27, ran into a running battle with Russian tanks, fell into a bomb crater near Elley and had to be given up. PZ 51, called in from the east, and PZ 26, summoned from Riga, took part in the fighting around Mitau, but on August 6 they were ordered to move to the Valk-Pleskow line in Estonia. On August 13 both trains met a Soviet tank attack near Somerpalu; PZ 51 was derailed and could not be helped by PZ 26, so it was blown up. PZ 26 returned to Valk. On August 16 a counterattack began, intended to restore the connection to Army Group North. PZ 3 and 21 were supposed to take part, but PZ 3 was derailed in transit and did not arrive. PZ 21 took part in the fighting from Mosheiken in the direction of Autz and was able to break the encircling ring in a narrow strip along the coast from Tukkum to Riga. Since Mitow remained in Russian hands, a connection between the lines had to be built west of that city, out of Libow and Vindow. This work, as well as the line through the Riga area, were secured by PZ 26.

The Army Group North Ukraine (that was Army Group South's name since March 30, 1944; Army Group A became Army Group South Ukraine at that time) met a Russian advance from Tarnopol on July 14. PZ 63, sent to attack partisans in the area northeast of Lemberg early in May by Army Group North, was on the Stanislav-Buczacz line since June 5, and was called immediately, joining the battle ahead of Krasne. But on July 17 it met its fate at the small depot in Kutkorz. T-34 tanks broke through along the line and suddenly opened fire on the train (this method, demoralizing and costly for the armored train, was used by the Soviets again and again from then on). A real Odyssey ensued for PZ 11. On July 17 it set out to the north with Armored Engines 16 and 18 (PT 16 was supposed to join PZ 63, which was not possible because of the latter's loss), and was able to escape encirclement in Rava Russka; it suffered heavy losses in battle near Zamosc and finally reached Lublin. From there it was able to escape capture on July 24—though losing one car and its locomotive—and move in the direction of the San. On July 27-28 it defended the San crossing at Rozvadov, again suffering losses. Further retreat took it—still with both engines—through Mielec (August 3-5) to Debica; after the front was stabilized it went to Krakow for repairs. The Russian breakthrough across the Bug west of Kovel had a particularly fatal effect on the south wing of Army Group Center. On July 16-17 the Soviets had reached the Bug north of Brest-Litovsk. Counterattacks were made from the only remaining German bridgehead at Platerov, supported by PZ 66 on July 21-25. When the Russians advanced northward from the Vlodava-Lublin area, they threatened the railway from Warsaw to Brest-Litovsk. PZ 68 was still able to teach Lukov on July 24, but had to retreat from the advancing Russians to Siedlice [p. 40] and take part in its defense. On July 26 the Russians broke the rail line east of Siedlice. PZ 66, called in from the Bug bridgehead, could no longer keep it open and had to be blown up four days later after running out of ammunition. Since Siedlice itself was in danger of being surrounded, PZ 68 was sent northward on July 28. On July 29 it set out from Tlusczcz to attack in the direction of Volomin, and then spent the next month covering the Bug crossing near Vyszkow. The Russians had also come dangerously close to the Armored Train Replacement Unit's base in Rembertov (east of Warsaw), and it was moved to Milovitz (east of Prague) on July 23-26. Two armored trains that were being

*PZ 74 had the shortest career. Hastily and not completely prepared, it was sent into action on July 25, 1944, only to be shot down southeast of Warsaw on July 29.*

PZ 21 lost its armored locomotive in battle at Vilna on July 8, 1944 and was pulled by an unarmored military locomotive (52 6233) from then until its end on October 31.

equipped at Rembertov but were not yet finished had to rush into action: PZ 74 was assigned to the 73rd Infantry Division, which was to take a defensive position near Garvolin on the line to Deblin southeast of Warsaw, but it was thrown back to Otvok on July 27. Two days later PZ 74 was shot down by Russian tanks near Pogorzel; its four days were the shortest "career" of any armored train. PZ 75 advanced eastward from Rembertov and dropped back to Praga, the eastern suburb of Warsaw, on July 30. There the nearness of the Red Army inspired an uprising, which broke out on August 1. PZ 75 took part in the successful defense of the vistula bridge and supported the forces who moved against the rebels from the rail ring, at first from the east side, later from the north. This had a grim effect on the Poles, but prevented the blowing up of the lines that brought reinforcements into the inner city from the western and northern suburbs. PZ 75 (renamed Armored Instructional Train 5 at the end of August, as it was meant to be a training train for the Replacement Unit) stayed in Warsaw until the end of September. Then it was joined by the newly arrived PZ 30 and a railway protection train to form a barrage line between Zyradov and Yaktorov (west of Warsaw), where it

came upon and wiped out a partisan group encircled in the woods south of the Vistula on September 29. Then both trains were given securing tasks in the area between Lavich-Petrikow and Warsaw. As of October 21 they (PZ 30 had been joined by PT 19) were in action in the Nasielsk-Modlin area before the Narev bridgehead.

In mid-May 1944 PZ 71, after being updated, had been sent to the Army Group South Ukraine (ex-A) in Galatz, Romania, to secure their supply lines. After the Russian offensive against that group (August 20), PZ 71 returned to Ploesti and was to go on through the Predeal Pass to Kronstadt. It was stopped in Ploesti, though, and sent to Slanic to pick up a Luftwaffe staff. This sealed its fate, for on August 29 the Russians had already reached Ploesti and cut off its return route, so that it had to be blown up on August 31. The fall of Romania inspired another rebellion. On August 27 the German military mission, on [p. 41] its way back from Romania to St. Martin, was captured and shot by Slovak partisans. This moved units of the Slovakian Army to rebel, but they could be limited to the central Slovakian area fairly soon. On September 1 PZ 62 arrived on the Kaschau-Preschau line from the eastern edge of the rebel area. Apparently it took part in the opening of the railroad line from the east (Deutschendorf) in the Waag valley, reaching Rosenberg as early as September 9. The section from Rosenberg to Sillein (and thus the establishment of through east-west transit) took longer; it was only fully usable on October 11, and PZ 62 was still securing its eastern section in mid-October, with PT 20 assigned to it. The Slovaks had also built three armored trains, which fell into German hands by the end of October, after the rebellion had been put down, and of which two railway protection trains were assembled. Early in November PZ 22 (with PT 22), transferred in from France, replaced PZ 62 for track securing in Slovakia; the latter was transferred to the Army

In August 1944 the rebuilt PZ 30 (tank-destroyer car, German gun turrets, new armored locomotive (below), along with Armored Engine 19 (above), was sent to the area west of Warsaw.

After the Allies took over France, the armored trains stationed there (PZ 22, 24 and 25) were transferred to Army Group A on the eastern front in October and November 1944, some after being rearmed. PZ 22 (with its subordinated engine PT 22) is seen here in Slovakia.

Group South's territory (on September 24 another renaming had been done; the Army Group South Ukraine was simply called "South", while "North Ukraine" became Army Group A) for securing, probably taking part in the defensive fighting near Miskolc. When the Soviets broke through into the Slovakian-Hungarian border area at the juncture of the 1st Hungarian and 8th Armies, it was damaged in the defensive fighting in the Gross-Steffelsdorf-Füllek area and then was sent back to Army Group A in Poland. In late October and early November, other armored trains, PZ 24 and 25, reached Poland from the west, after much of France had been occupied by the Allies. At first they were used for securing in the area south of Krakow. With them, the long-planned command of the armored trains could finally establish Regimental Staff No. 2 (Oberstleutnant von Türckheim, with Command Train 72A) with Army Group A in Krakow. In the subordinated 1st Armored Train Battalion, a unit with PZ 24 and 62 (the PT 20 engine belonging to this train was away—for the duration of the war—for repairs) was stationed in Jelen (Koluszki-Skarzysko line) toward the end of the year, and another with PZ 11 and 25 plus PT 16 and 18 south of Kielce; PZ 22 with PT 22 remained the only train in Slovakia for a time.

On October 5 the Red Army had also become active in the north. In only five days it broke through the 3rd Armored Army to the Baltic Sea, thus separating Army Group North from the rest of the front permanently. PZ 21, remaining unchanged in the Moscheiken-Autz area, had been joined by PZ 3 on the line from Moscheiken toward Schaulen. The latter got into combat on October 5 and fought its way back to Moscheiken. But the Russians had penetrated to the north

and threatened the line from Libau to there. PZ 3 was thus moved to Weinoden on October 7 and tried in vain to open the line to Moscheiken, with PZ 21 in action from the other side. When Weinoden was also cut off from the west and the Russians threatened to capture it, PZ 3 was blown up on October 10. PZ 21 later suffered the same fate in Moscheiken, after supporting the defense of the city until October 31. PZ 26 stayed in the Army Group North area (later Courland). After it had secured the transport of troops from Riga to Tukkum, it was sent to the Libau line, on which the developing combat pushed it ever farther back until the surrender on May 8, 1945.

Since the Soviets had reached the Memel in their October offensive, the new PZ 52, a rebuilt railway protection train (with PT 21) was sent to Tilsit to secure the crossing there. On October 16 the Soviets broke into East Prussia from the Schirwindt-Suwalki area, reaching the Gumbinnen-Goldap line on October 22. PZ 52 was brought in from the north, and PZ 68, which had been at the Narev crossing near Ostrolenka since September, from the south. Above all, though, the Regimental Commander, Oberstleutnant Dr. Günther, and his Command Train 72B reached the Army Group Center to command the armored trains. The three armored trains took part in the recapturing of Goldap early in November. Later PZ 30 (with PT 19) and PLZ 5, then at the Narev brodgehead in Nasielsk, were called to East Prussia. Of the two armored train battalions, one always operated from then on from Treuburg toward Goldap, the other to the east. On December 1 PLZ 5 was replaced by the new PZ 75 (with PT 23) and could then begin its planned use as a training train with the Replacement Unit, though

In October 1944 the rebuilt PZ 52, made from the railway protection train "Blücher", wa sent to East Prussia and took part in the recapture of Goldap.

*Soviet armored trains were also active (here in the summer of 1944), but were only seen when the line of battle remained stable for a long time (which was the case less and less often), as they had to wait until the railways had been adapted for broad gauge until just behind the front. (PM)*

for only a few weeks. At the end of the year PZ 68 had to be sent to Königsberg for repairs, while PT 21 was sent back to Germany for the same reason.

On December 1 the Soviets began their major offensive against Army Groups A and Center. The armored wedge ahead of the Baranov bridgehead was aimed fairly accurately at the location of the armored train battalion south of Kielce. On January 13 PZ 11 and 25 were put out of action and had to be given up. The damaged PT 18 could get away to Kielce but not escape from there; only PT 16 could break through to the south to take part in combat in the Upper Silesian industrial area before being withdrawn for repairs. When the Red Army advanced from the Pulavy bridgehead on that day, the other armored train battalion (PZ 24 and 62), stationed at Tomaszov, was alerted and sent to the Radom area; there was no enemy action there or on the trip back to Skarzysko Kamienna. The rest of the line was crowded with evacuation trains, and accidents caused by haste caused further delays. When they wanted to leave Volka Piebanska in the direction of Konskie, the news came that the Russians had already reached the next depot, and their tanks advancing along the line had shot down the trains. Thus the battalion commander had the trains, which had not fired a shot, blown up, while the crews retreated on foot. Only Command Train 72A with the regimental commander had been able to leave Krakow and reach Silesia in time. The Russians also moved against East Prussia. While one arm of the pincers advanced toward Königsberg between Memel and Ebenrode, the other turned from the Narev bridgehead toward the lower Vistula. The armored trains of Regiment 3 (Oberstleutnant Dr. Günther), stationed with the 4th Army, remained unendangered at first and were alerted only on January 19. PZ 30 and 72B were sent via Allenstein to Deutsch-Eylau. On a scouting trip toward Soldau, they met the Russian spearhead near

Hartowitz; PT 19 was damaged but could be towed away. They withdrew to Deutsch-Eylau, where the finished part of PZ 68 (two gun cars and the armored locomotive stayed behind) had arrived, accompanying a transport train from Königsberg to Marienburg. When Deutsch-Eylau was surrounded by the Russians, they retreated in the direction of Marienburg on January 22-23, taking as many refugees as possible, and crossed the Nogat going west on January 25. The regiment's other two armored trains, PZ 52 and 76, were ordered to Königsberg, but only PZ 76 (with PT 23) followed this order and went into service east of the city; PZ 52 went west via Bartenstein and was able to cross the Nogat at Marienburg before the line was cut by the Russians. PZ 76 went back to Königsberg and onto the line to Fischhausen, remaining [p. 43] outside the ring that enclosed Königsberg. It took part in opening the blockade on February 20. The rest of PZ 68, which had stayed in Königsberg, had meanwhile been finished and was attached to PT 23. This unit was in the city during the final Russian attack, and took part in the defensive fighting to the bitter end, first at the main depot, then at the north station. PZ 76 was destroyed at Seerappen. The remaining trains of Dr. Günther's regimental battle group (PZ 30, 52, 68 and 72B) saw action first on the Vistula front opposite Graudenz, then on the Konitz-Czersk-Preussisch Stargard line.

Once again the army groups had been renamed: Army Group North, cut off in the Baltic area, was now called "Courland", the part of Army Group Center cut off in East Prussia became "North", Army Group A in Silesia and Moravia was "Center", and into the "empty" area in Pomerania and along the Oder, which the Soviets reached via Küstrin on January 31, the new Army Group Vistula was sent. All available troops had to be gathered to form this group, including the armored train group to be formed on the Oder front. For it, only the railway protection trains "Max"

*PZ 65, with the replacement unit in the Balkans after being damaged, was quickly repaired (above, note the freight car rebuilt as a command car and the unusual gun car behind it— with 2 cm AA gun quads in "Wirbelwind" turrets) and sent to the Oder front early in February 1945, after the Red Army had advanced to that river.*

and No. 83 and the engines 22 and 37 were available at first. They were commanded by the von Türckheim regimental staff, which had lost all its trains in Poland. A makeshift command train (No. II) was added, so that the former one (72A) could serve as a combat train. The group gained further strength from the overhauled PZ 65, which replaced the protection train "Max", the railway protection train "Berlin" "donated" by the Ministry of Armaments and the Inspector General of the Armored Troops (five undriveable "Panther" tanks set on flatcars), and Armored Engines 16 and 21. These vehicles were on the Münchberg-Werbig-Küstrin and Fürstenwalde-Rosengarten-Frankfurt on the Oder lines, as well as the Werbig-Rosengarten connecting line, to attack the Russian Oder bridgeheads. An armored train battalion in Pomerania was also subordinated to the regimental staff; it consisted of Armored Training Train 5, now a combat train again, and the new PZ 77. The latter covered the withdrawal from beyond Arnswalde to Stargard, the second that from Pyritz to there. Both also took part in the counterattack out of Arnsberg in mid-February, but it soon came to a stop. On February 24 the Soviets began their offensive against Pomerania. PZ 77 defended the Bublitz

depot against a Russian tank attack, but when it tried to do so again the next day it ran into a tank trap and was destroyed. PZ 72A, called from the Oder front, replaced it. It and PLZ 5 operated in the Belgard-Köslin area. P Z72A withdrew to Kolberg before its area was surrounded and took part in the defense of that city until its surrender on March 16. PLZ 5 was cut off in Belgard and blown up on March 4. The crew was able to reached the German lines after a week's adventurous march. [p. 44] The Russian breakthrough in Pomerania had the worst results for Dr. Günther's regimental group's armored trains (PZ 30, 52, 68 and 72B) southwest of Dirschau. This has been ordered on February 27 to join Army Group Center in the Bautzen-Görlitz area. By request of the 2nd Army, its departure was delayed by one day. Thus the armored trains encountered the Russians west of Schlawe, as they had broken through to the Baltic on March 1. They had blown up the bridge over the Grabow, and there was nothing for the regimental group to do but head back eastward to the Gotenhafen area. The armored trains served as battalions in the Gross-Katz area. When PZ 30 and 52 were on the front, a bridge was blown up behind them during a Russian advance, and they were

*Early in February 1945 the new PZ 77 reached Pomerania, only to be destroyed near Bublitz on February 27.*

captured by the Soviets on March 21. PZ 68 and 72A went to Gotenhafen, and after it fell on March 28 they moved to the Oxhöfter Kampe, where they were blown up. The Army Group Center had summoned PZ 22, the last remaining armored train, from Slovakia to Silesia in February. It saw action first at the Oder bridgehead near Steinau north of Breslau (a cobbled-up armored train was also active in that city during the surrounding), and on February 11 it was destroyed by Russian tanks at Sprottau.

As 1945 began, Hitler turned his special interest to Hungary. Thus PZ 64, which had been at Barcs since the 2nd Armored Army had joined Army Group South on December 1, 1944 in withdrawing from Fünfkirchen, was joined by the new PZ 78 and 79 early in February; all three covered the lines from the southwest corner of the Plattensee to Somogyszob and from Gyekenyes to Vizvar, behind which were the oilfields near Nagykanisza. When the Russians advanced north of the Plattensee in mid-March, PZ 79 was to move into the penetration area on the Sarvar-Papa line. It was outflanked and destroyed by the Soviets west of Czeldömölk on March 27. PZ 78 was also moved to the north shore of the Plattensee, but returned to Nagykanisza. PZ 64 and 78 were able to cross the Drau early in April and reach southern Styria. In the last weeks of the war they were east of Spielfeld, withdrawing via Graz at the surrender. PZ 78 still reached the area of Judenburg; PZ 64 remained in Pernegg (before Bruck), and PT 19, assigned to it shortly before the end, went on toward Leoben.

The last act of the drama on the eastern front began with a tremendous fusillade on the morning of April 16, behind which the Russians advanced on both sides of Küstrin.

A focal point of their attack was the Seelow Heights. The armored train "Berlin" was near Seelow, advanced to the rail triangle east of Werbig, and is said to have shot down no fewer than 56 Soviet tanks from the causeway and bridge. On the other hand, it could not get to the line leading to Münchberg, and since the Russians had advanced to the railway lines farther south, near Ludwigslust and Dolgelin, the train, already damaged by artillery fire and low-flying planes, had to be abandoned. The other armored trains (PZ 65 and 83, with PT 16, 21 and 22) were in the Rosengarten area and took part in the fighting around Schönfliess. The front could be held in that area. On April 19, still before the Russians advancing from the north could block the line near Fürstenwalde, the armored trains set out toward Berlin and from there on to Mecklenburg. On April 24 they were in Waren on the Müritzsee. On April 17 railway protection train 350 was finished in Berlin; it was sent to Bad Freienwalde, the northernmost point of the 9th Army, but had to move to Eberswalde two days later. [p. 45] There it reached the Steiner Army Unit, from which the relief of Berlin from the north was expected. With it, the train left for the area north of Oranienburg on April 24, where PT 16 and 22 arrived the same day. Their own attempted attacks soon failed; instead they had to defend against the advancing Soviets at Oranienburg and Kremmen. On April 27 PZ 350 and PT 16 were withdrawn from Beetz-Sommerfeld toward Neu-Ruppin; PT 22 left one day later from Neustadt on the Dosse toward Rhinow-Rathenow, before the gates of which the Russians already were. In March another armored train, PZ 75, had reached the area south of Berlin from the Balkans. It was between Golssen and Baruth, thus right on

*PZ 64 was south of the Plattensee in Hungary in March 1945.*

*Last hours of the armored trains: On the day after the final Russian offensive began, on April 17, 1945, Railway Protection Train 350, built up into an armored train (above) reached the Oder front. Note the Pzner IVH tank without running gear but with aprons set on a flatcar. Below: the rebuilt PZ 7 heads for action near Olmütz in Moravia late in April 1945.*

the advance route of the Soviet 3rd Armored Army after their breakthrough between Cottbus and Spremberg. On April 19 it moved south of Baruth to delay their advance a little, but their advance to the southern edge of Berlin was unstoppable. PZ 75 supplied rear-guard action near Gross-Beeren on April 22, and was able to move westward via Spandau safely before the line was broken near Nauen. On April 30 it supposed a last German counterattack attempt from Friesack in the direction of Brädikow. On the same day PZ 75 and 350, plus PT 22, gathered in Neustadt on the Dosse and departed in the direction of Wittenberge (PT 16, damaged, stayed behind in Neustadt). PZ 65 and 83 and PT 21 were in the Karow-Parchim area on that day. On May 2 all the units gathered in Neustadt-Glewe and moved together through Ludwigslust toward Schwerin, meeting the Americans in Holthusen and surrendering to them. The regimental commander with Command Train II— with the army group staff southwest of Prenzlau since early March—got away toward Waren before the Russians took Prenzlau on April 27. From there they tried to find their own way via Goldberg-Bad Kleinen, but the lines were filled west of Grevesmühlen, so on May 2 they left the train and disbanded the unit. In what remained in German hands of Bohemia and Moravia at the war's end, the Armored Train Replacement Uniit was located in Milowitz. Here armored trains were equipped to the end. These were PZ 80 and 81 of the standard BP 44 series (PZ 82 was never completed), the rebuilt PZ 7 and 27, as well as a somewhat ominous PZ 99, the railway protection train "Moritz', the heavy armored scout trains no. 205 and 206, and PT 36. As May began, a regimental staff was even formed, using the makeshift Command Train III. Little is known of the activities of these trains. PZ 80, replaced by PZ 7 on April 25, was in action west of Olmütz. The latter remained in Bohemian Trübau, the first

was able to cross the Moldau. On May 3 the Czechs rose up against the occupying forces. Fighting against irregular forces is the domain of the armored trains. That it was avoided and trains were even abandoned withoput dire becessity shows how morale had sunk when the war's coming end was in sight. According to Czech sources, armored trains were captured at the following places: Iglau, north of Kralup, Oberleutensdorf, Lissa (Armored Scout Train 205 and one other), Milowitz (Armored Scout Train 206 and the unfinished PZ 82); one other must have stopped near Reichenburg. Like many others, the armored train troops, including the replacement unit, tried to reach the American lines but did not have the luck of their comrades in Mecklenburg. The 3rd US Army had given their commanders strict orders not to let anyone cross the demarcation line. So none of the Germans who arrived there could avoid the fate of being taken prisoner by the Russians.

# The Division of Armored Trains Among the Army Groups on the Eastern Front

| Army Group North As of 6/22/1941 | Army Group Center | Army Group South | |
|---|---|---|---|
| 6, 26, 30 | 1, 2, 3, 27, 28, 29 | 4, 7, 31 | |
| | late 10/41 3 repaired | | |
| | 1/2/42 27 lost | | |
| | 1/10/42 29 lost | | |
| | 1/15/42 28 left>>> | 1/15/42 28 came | |
| | | 1/15/42 10 new came | |
| | 2/22/42 27 new came | | |
| | early 3/42 3 came | | |
| 5/42 6 gone, rebuilt | 5/22/42 25 new came | | |
| | 5/28/42 3 repaired | | |
| | 5/30/42 27 rebuilt | | |
| | 7/1/42 4 came <<< | 7/1/42 4 left | |
| | | **7/6/42 Army Group B** | |
| 8/42 51 new came | | | |
| | 10/10/42 3 came | | |
| | 10/10/42 25 >France | | |
| | 10/10/42 21 <France | | |
| 11/42 30 rebuilt | 11/42 27 new came | 11/2/42 31 rebuilt | **11/24/42 Army Group Don** |
| | | 11/23/42 7, 10 left> | 11/24/42 7, 10 came |
| | 12/14/42 1 rebuilt | | |
| 1/43 26 rebuilt | 12/23/42 61 new came | 12/23/42 28 left > | 12/23/42 28 came |
| | | | 2/18/43 62 new came |
| | | **2/23/42 Army Group South** | |
| early 5/43 3 rebuilt | | | |
| | 7/13/43 3 rebuilt | | |
| | 8/17/43 66 new came | 8/11/43 11 came (ex-10 II) | |
| | 8/23/43 1 new came | | |
| | early 10/43 67 new came | mid 10/43 31 new came | |
| | | **Army Group A (since 7/6/42)** | |
| | early 11/43 68 new came | 11/16/43 69 new came | |
| | 11/9/43 4 rebuilt 11/18/43 62 left> | 11/18/43 62 came | |
| | | 12/21/43 70 new came | |
| | | 12/28/43 31 lost | |
| | | 1/44 7, 28 rebuilt | |
| 1/10/44 67 came< | < 1/10/44 67 left | 1/11/44 62 came | <1/11/44 62 left |
| | | 1/12/44 71 new came | |
| 2/20/44 26 new came | | 2/10/44 71 R/60 came | <EA 2/21/44 30 new came |
| | | **3/20/44 Army Group North-Ukraine** | |
| | | | **3/20/44 Army Group South-Ukraine** |
| | | 3/21/44 69 lost | |
| | | 3/22/44 R/60 lost | |
| | | late 3/44 10 lost | |
| 3/31/44 71 came < | <late 3/44 71 left | | |
| | late 3/44 27 lost | 4/4/44 70 lost | |
| | | late 4/44 11 repaired | 4/13/44 30 repaired |
| | | late 4/44 63 came (< A.Gr.North) | |
| | 5/11/44 70 left> | | >5/15/44 71 came |
| | 5/44 28 new came | | |
| | early 6/44 2 rebuilt | | |
| | 6/27/44 1, 61 lost | | |
| | 6/29/44 28 lost [page 47 | | |

| Army Group North | Army Group Center | Army Gr. N.-Ukraine | Army Gr. S.-Ukraine |
|---|---|---|---|
|  | 7/18/44 3 new came | 7/17/44 63 lost |  |
|  | 7/25/44 74, 75 new came | 7/17/44 11 new came |  |
| 7/27/44 67 lost | 7/29/44 74 lost |  |  |
|  | 7/30/44 66 lost |  |  |
| 8/13/44 51 lost | 8/28/44 30 new came |  | 8/31/44 71 lost |
|  |  | **9/25/44 Army Group A** | **9/25/44 Army Gr. South** |
|  | 10/10/44 52 new came | late 9/44 62 left> | >late 9/44 62 came |
|  | 10/10/44 3 lost |  |  |
|  | 10/21/44 72b new came | 10/23/44 24 came <France |  |
|  | 10/30/44 21 lost | early 11/44 22 came <France |  |
|  |  |  | 11/12/44 64 came <Balkans |
|  |  | late 11/44 25 came <France |  |
|  | 12/1/44 L5 left >EA | late 11/44 72a new came (St.2) |  |
|  | 12/1/44 76 new came | 12/44 62 came < | <12/44 62 left |
|  |  | 1/13/45 11, 25 lost |  |
|  |  | 1/16/45 24, 62 lost |  |

**1/25/45 A.Gr.Courland** [nothing listed until bottom line]

| **1/25/45 A.Gr. North** | **1/25/45 A.Gr.Vistula** | **1/25/45 A/Gr/Center** |  |
|---|---|---|---|
|  | 1/29/45 L5 came (<EA) |  |  |
|  | 2/2/45 72a came < | <2/2/45 72a left |  |
|  | 2/2/45 77, 83 new came |  |  |
|  | 2/3/45 Com.II new came (St.2) |  | 2/6/45 78 new came |
|  | 2/6/45 65 came (<Balkans) |  | 2/6/45 79 new came |
|  | 2/15/45 Berlin new came | 2/11/45 22 lost |  |
|  | 2/27/45 77 lost |  |  |
|  | 3/5/45 L5 lost |  |  |
| 3/21/45 30, 52 lost | 3/16/45 72a lost | late 3/45 80 new came |  |
| 3/28/45 68, 72b lost | mid-3/45 75 came (<Balkans) | late 3/45 27 new came | 3/27/45 79 lost |
| 4/14/45 76 lost | 4/16/45 Berlin lost |  |  |
|  | 4/17/45 350 new came | late 4/45 Com III came (St.3) |  |
|  |  | late 4/45 81 new came |  |
|  |  | early 5/45 new 7 came |  |
|  |  | early 5/45 new 205, 206 came |  |

On Hand as of capitulation, early May 1945

| [A.Gr.Courland] | {A.Gr. North} |  |  |
|---|---|---|---|
| 26 | none |  |  |
|  | 65, 75, 83, 350, Com II | 7, 27, 80, 81, Com III, 205, 206, others? | 64, 78 |

**To the following armored trains on the eastern front, armored engines were subordinated:**

PZ 25  PT 15 (5/22-9/42)
PZ 61  PT 17 (late 12/43-6/17/44 lost)
PZ 11  PT 16 (6/44-1/13/45), PT 18 (7/44-1/13/45, 1/16/45 lost)
PZ 30  PT 19 (8/44-1/45)
PZ 62  PT 20 (9/44-12/44)
PZ 52  PT 21 (10/44-12/44)
PZ 22  PT 22 (10/44-late 1/45)
PZ 76  PT 23 (11/44-4/45 lost)
PZ 64  PT 19 (4/45-5/9/45)

The Armored Train Battle Group of Army Group Vistula (PZ 65, 72a, 83, Berlin, 350) had (the exact details are unknown): PT 16 (as of 2/20/45; 4/23/45 with PZ 350), PT 21 (since early 3/45), PT 22 (since 2/2/45); with Army Group South from end of 2/45 to capitulation were PT 15, PT 19, PT 20 was being repaired at RAW Nuremberg in 4/45.

**Code:**

came: arrived at that army group
Com: command train
EA: armored train replacement unit
left: departed from that army group
lost: destroyed or abandoned
new: newly built, much rebuilt or newly reconstituted
rebuilt: left to be rebuilt
repaired: left to be repaired (major repairs only)
St. (armored train regimental staff)
< > arrows indicate movement from one group to another

Note: In 1945 upgraded railway protection trains 83, 350 and "Berlin" became armored trains.

# Epilogue

Thus the war against the Soviet Union, begun on June 22, 1941, ended with the defeat of the German Army and German Reich. It was actually lost already when none of the planned goals had been attained by the winter of 1941-42. Leningrad had been surrounded and Kharkov taken, but the forces were halted before Moscow and had been hit hard at Rostov even before the Russian counteroffensive began. They were far from the planned Archangel-Astrakhan securing line. Above all, they had not forced the Red Army to its knees despite its heavy losses. Stalin did not have to withdraw behind the Urals to continue the war—now that he had the potent USA, on which Hitler had declared war, on his side—and his winter offensive against the Germans, who were hit hard by the mud season, the ensuing extreme cold and the unexpected tough resistance of the Soviets, was very effective. They could be stopped only with tough fighting and many losses of men and materials. In the end their will was broken, and the Germans' main problem, namely that they did not have anywhere near sufficient forces to occupy the front and hinterland permanently, became evident. To continue the war on the eastern front successfully, their only chance would have been to try to get the native populations, who had seen the Germans at first as liberators from Communism, on their side actively. But the National Socialist racial policy was diametrically opposed to this, driving them into the arms of Stalin's "Great National War" and making them fanatical fighters for their homeland's cause. The apparent success of the 1942 summer offensive only made the problems worse: The Red Army dropped back, saving its entire strength for the counteroffensive, the front line became extremely thin, and finally, even thos advance could not achieve any of the planned goals (Caucasian Black Sea coast, oil fields, Stalingrad). The bitter end could be seen then at the latest, even though it dragged out over two years, with tremendous losses on both sides. Instead of gaining territory in the east for Germany, the Soviet and Communist area of influence extended into central Europe, to the Elbe and the Bohemian Forest as well as much of the Balkans, and instead of winning "living space for the German master race", all the areas of settlement east of that border, in which some 18 million Germans had lived—often for centuries—were removed from the map, resulting in eviction and migration (which continues for the Russian Germans to this day).

*PZ 6 is seen with Army Group North in the Dno-Batezkaya-Staraya Russa-Novgorod area during the winter of 1941-42. (KM)*

*An interesting picture from Rembertow in the spring of 1944: At left is the armored Diesel locomotive WR 360 C 14, which pulled PZ 83 when the war ended, then a captured Soviet armored locomotive, the model for the armoring of Series 57 of BP 42 and 44, which was assigned to PZ 30 in August 1944; behind it is a car from PZ 10, liberated in Kovel but badly damaged.*